THE RHODODENDRONS OF SIKKIM-HIMALAYA

BEING
AN ACCOUNT, BOTANICAL AND GEOGRAPHICAL, OF THE RHODODENDRONS RECENTLY DISCOVERED IN THE MOUNTAINS OF EASTERN HIMALAYA

JOSEPH DALTON HOOKER, R. N., M. D., F. R. S., F. L. S.
EDITED BY
SIR W. J. HOOKER, K. H., D. C. L., F. R. A. S., & L. S.

GYAN

Published by

Gyan Publishing House
5, Ansari Road
Daryaganj, New Delhi-110002
Phone: 011-47034999, 9811692060
E-mail: books@gyanbooks.com

Distribution Network
gyanbooks.com
India, USA, Canada, UK, Australia, France

ISBN: 978-81-212-8390-8 (PB)
First Published, 1849

2nd Impression 2023

Printed at: Gyan Press, Delhi.

THE RHODODENDRONS OF SIKKIM-HIMALAYA
Author: JOSEPH DALTON HOOKER

THE RHODODENDRONS OF SIKKIM-HIMALAYA

Tab. I.

J.D.H. del. Fitch, lith.

Reeve, Benham & Reeve, imp.

RHODODENDRON DALHOUSIÆ, Hook. fil.

(in its native locality)

THE

RHODODENDRONS

OF

SIKKIM-HIMALAYA;

BEING

AN ACCOUNT, BOTANICAL AND GEOGRAPHICAL, OF THE RHODODENDRONS RECENTLY DISCOVERED IN THE MOUNTAINS OF EASTERN HIMALAYA,

FROM

DRAWINGS AND DESCRIPTIONS MADE ON THE SPOT,

DURING A GOVERNMENT BOTANICAL MISSION TO THAT COUNTRY;

BY

JOSEPH DALTON HOOKER, R.N., M.D., F.R.S., F.L.S.,

&c., &c., &c.

EDITED BY

SIR W. J. HOOKER, K.H., D.C.L., F.R.A.S. & L.S.,

Vice-President of the Linnæan Society, and Director of the Royal Gardens of Kew.

SECOND EDITION.

KINCHIN-JUNGA (Elev. 28,178 ft.) as seen from DARJEELING.

LONDON:

REEVE, BENHAM, AND REEVE, KING WILLIAM STREET, STRAND.

1849.

TO

HER ROYAL HIGHNESS,

THE PRINCESS MARY OF CAMBRIDGE,

WHOSE TASTE FOR THE PLEASURES OF A GARDEN,

THE FIRST AND PUREST PLEASURES OF OUR RACE, HAS MADE HER FEEL PECULIAR INTEREST IN

The Great National Establishment at Kew,

AND WHO,

CONJOINTLY WITH HER ROYAL PARENTS,

HAS EVER BEEN FORWARD IN PROMOTING WHATEVER MIGHT TEND TO ITS USEFULNESS AND EMBELLISHMENT,

THE FOLLOWING FIGURES AND DESCRIPTIONS

OF A SERIES OF EMINENTLY BEAUTIFUL PLANTS, DESTINED SHORTLY TO ADD NEW LUSTRE TO ITS TREASURES,

ARE MOST HUMBLY DEDICATED,

BY HER ROYAL HIGHNESS' DUTIFUL AND OBEDIENT SERVANT,

THE EDITOR.

Royal Gardens, Kew,
March 15th, 1849.

PREFACE.

DARJEELING, in the Sikkim portion of the Himalaya, the native country of the plants figured and described in the following pages, is situated in lat. 27° N., and long. the same as Calcutta, from which it is distant about 380 miles. Its elevation above the sea is 7,200 feet. The mean temperature of the year is about 55° of Fahrenheit, and that of each month, as detailed in a Calendar communicated by Dr. Campbell, the Hon. the E. I. C. Resident at Darjeeling, to the late Lord Auckland, and now lying before me, is as follows:—

January	41°	May	59°	September	61° 50′
February	43°	June	64°	October	58° 50′
March	53° 50′	July	65°	November	48°
April	57°	August	65°	December	44°

"In five years," further observes Dr. Campbell, "there have been three heavy falls of snow: one in December, 1842; one in January, 1839; and one in February, 1841."

The mountain Sinchul, upon a spur of which, looking north, Darjeeling stands, attains an elevation of 9,000 feet, and to the west of it, next Nepal, rises another conspicuous mountain, Tonglo, reaching a height of 10,000 feet. Due north of Darjeeling, at a distance of only sixty miles, the horizon is bounded by the great snowy range (as seen, or rather attempted to be shown, in the vignette of the title-page), having for its principal feature the peak of KINCHIN-JUNGA, which has lately been ascertained to be 28,172 feet in elevation, the loftiest mountain yet known in the world. Dr. Hooker thus describes his first impressions of this scene:—"Much as I had heard and read of the magnificence and beauty of Himalayan scenery, my highest expectations have been surpassed! I arrived at Darjeeling on a rainy misty day, which did not allow me to see ten yards in any direction, much less to descry the Snowy Range, distant sixty miles in a straight line. Early next morning I caught my first view, and I literally held my breath in awe and admiration. Six or seven successive ranges of forest-clad mountains, as high as that whereon I stood (8,000 feet), intervened between me and a dazzling white pile of snow-clad mountains, among which the giant peak of Kinchin-junga rose 20,000 feet *above* the lofty point from which I gazed! Owing to the clearness of the atmosphere, the snow appeared, to my fancy, but a few miles off, and the loftiest mountain at only a day's journey. The heavenward outline was projected against a pale blue sky; while little detached patches of mist clung here and there to the highest peaks, and were tinged golden yellow, or rosy red, by the rising sun, which touched these elevated points long ere it reached the lower position which I occupied.

B

"Such is the aspect of the Himalaya range at early morning. As the sun's rays dart into the many valleys which lie between the snowy mountains and Darjeeling, the stagnant air contained in the low recesses becomes quickly heated: heavy masses of vapour, dense, white, and keenly defined, arise from the hollows, meet over the crests of the hills, cling to the forests on their summits, enlarge, unite, and ascend rapidly to the rarefied regions above,—a phenomenon so suddenly developed, that the consequent withdrawal from the spectator's gaze of the stupendous scenery beyond, looks like the work of magic." Such is the region of the Indian Rhododendrons.

Perhaps, with the exception of the Rose, the Queen of Flowers, no plants have excited a more lively interest throughout Europe than the several species of the genus *Rhododendron*,[1] whether the fine evergreen foliage be considered, or the beauty and profusion of the blossoms; and it may probably be said with truth, that no kind of flowering shrub is so easily, and has been so extensively, cultivated, or has formed so vast an article of traffic, as that one oriental species to which the name seems more immediately to have been given, the *Rhododendron Ponticum*. Its poisonous qualities, too, have tended to bring it the more into notice; for, to eating the honey collected by the bees from that plant, (as well as from the *Azalea Pontica*,) in the neighbourhood of Trebizond, during the celebrated retreat of the Ten Thousand, were attributed the dreadful sufferings of the Greeks; so severe that their actions were said to resemble those of drunken persons or madmen. Major Madden has stated that cattle sometimes perish by feeding upon the foliage and flowers of *Rhododendron arboreum* in the mountains of Kamaoon. Dr. Hooker remarks, on a recent tour while exploring the mountain-passes leading into Thibet:—"Here are three Rhododendrons, two of them resinous and strongly odoriferous; and it is to the presence of these plants that the natives attribute the painful sensations experienced at great elevations."

The *R. Ponticum*, which inhabits the mountains of Asia Minor and extends as far west as Spain and Portugal, together with *R. ferrugineum* and *hirsutum* of the European Alps, *R. Dahuricum* of Siberia, *R. Chamæcistus* of the Austrian and Piedmontese mountains, *R. maximum* of the United States of America, and the arctic *R. Lapponicum*, were all the kinds known to Linnæus and to the botanical world so recently as 1764. The beautiful *R. chrysanthum* of Northern Siberia appeared in Linnæus' Supplement. Gmelin added the *R. Kamtschaticum* from Okotsk and Behring's Straits, and Pallas the charming *R. Caucasicum* from the Caucasian Alps.

Towards the very close of the 18th century, namely in 1796, *R. arboreum*, the first of a new form and aspect of the genus, and peculiar to the lofty mountains of India Proper, was discovered by Captain Hardwicke, in the Sewalic chain of the Himalaya, while he was on a tour to Sireenagur. The species has since been found to have a very extended range. It was published in 1805 by Sir James E. Smith, in the "Exotic Botany" of that author, and is characterized by its arborescent stem, very rich scarlet flowers, and leaves that are silvery on the underside. Sir James, on the authority no doubt of Captain Hardwicke, gives the height of the tree at twenty feet; but Major Madden, who found it on the mountains of Kamaoon, at elevations of from 3,500 to 10,000 feet, says he might safely have doubled that measurement. On Binaur, a *trunk* was found to be thirteen feet in girth, and another at Nynee Tal, sixteen feet; while a third, at Singabee Devee, was fourteen feet and a half in the circumference of the stem at five feet from the ground.

[1] So called, as is well known, from ῥόδον, a *rose*, and δένδρον, a *tree*: a name, however, which was given with equal justice to the Rose-bay, *Nerium Oleander*, the ῥοδοδάφνη of the modern Greeks.

It does not appear on record by whom the *Tree Rhododendron* was first introduced into Europe, probably by Dr. Wallich, about the year 1827. We know that to that distinguished botanist we owe the discovery, and the possession of most of them in our gardens, of other noble Indian species, such as *R. formosum*, *R. barbatum*, *R. nobile*, *R. campanulatum*, *R. cinnamomeum*, with their many varieties, the limits of which are not clearly defined; and the facility these kinds afford for hybridizing with *R. arboreum*, thereby rendering the produce more hardy, has occasioned the original type of this latter species to be almost lost to our gardens.

R. Nilagiricum (Bot. Mag. t. 4381) was introduced to our gardens by Messrs. Lucombe, Pince, and Co., of the Exeter Nursery, a species assuredly quite, and permanently, distinct from *R. arboreum*, though published and figured under that name in Dr. Wight's *Icones*. Dr. Wallich, about the same period, detected another distinct, but not less interesting, group of species, in Northern India, more allied to *R. ferrugineum* and *R. hirsutum;* namely *R. setosum*, *R. lepidotum*, and *R. Anthopogon*.

Drs. Horsfield, Blume, and Jack made known some species from the mountains of Java: they were *R. Javanicum* (a most lovely shrub, introduced to our gardens by Messrs. Veitch and Sons of Exeter, through their collector, Mr. W. Lobb, see Bot. Mag. t. 4336), *R. album*, *R. retusum*, *R. tubiflorum*, *R. Malayanum*, and *R. Celebicum*. Blume, we believe, first noticed a species as being epiphytal, in Java ("supra arbores"), his *R.* (*Vireya*) *album*. Mr. William Lobb informs me that several kinds are there epiphytal; and Mr. Low, who speaks of the fine Rhododendrons existing in Borneo, particularizes one which inhabits invariably the trunks of trees, and which he had the good fortune to send to England alive, though we fear it has not been preserved in our collections.

What may be the number of species, or what the kinds, detected by Mr. Griffith during his travels in Bootan, we do not learn from the volume of his Posthumous Papers recently published at Calcutta by Mr. M'Clelland; nor am I aware whether Dr. Wight has published the whole of them in the paper of that gentleman, in the Calcutta Journal of Natural History, vol. viii., on certain Rhododendrons of Mr. Griffith. In Dr. Wight's Icones he figures and describes only two, *R. grande* and *R. Griffithianum;* both very distinct from any found by Dr. Hooker in the adjacent territory of Sikkim. And in proof of the prevalence of the genus in Bootan, it may be observed that Mr. Griffith, in his Journal, when speaking of one single excursion (to Doonglala Peak, 12,478 feet of elevation), enumerates no less than eight distinct species; viz.:—

* *Floribus in racemis umbelliformibus.*

1. *R. arboreum;* arboreum, foliis oblongo-obovatis subtus argenteis.
2. *R. ferrugineum;* arboreum, foliis obovatis supra rugosis subtus ferrugineis.
3. *R.* ——; fruticosum, foliis oblongis subtus ferrugineo-lepidotis.
4. *R. ellipticum;* fruticosum, foliis ellipticis.
5. *R.* ——; fruticosum, foliis ellipticis basi cordatis subtus glaucis reticulatis.
6. *R.* ——; fruticosum, foliis lanceolatis oblongis sub-obovatis subtus punctatis.
7. *R. undulatum;* fruticosum, foliis elongato-lanceolatis undulatis subtus reticulatis.

** *Floribus solitariis.*

8. *R. microphyllum;* fruticosum totum ferrugineo-lepidotum, foliis lanceolatis parvis.

B 2

In another place in Bootan (Pass of Rodoola, 12,000 feet), Mr. Griffith speaks of Rhododendrons as the only vegetation at the summit, and in the descent he traversed a "region of Rhododendrons."

It is not our intention, nor is it required by the nature of this little treatise, to enumerate all the Rhododendrons that are known in books: suffice it to say, that (exclusive of some Azaleas of Linnæus) thirty-two are distinguished by De Candolle in the seventh volume of his Prodromus, published in 1839; and enough has been here stated to show that the maximum of the species exists in Asia; for, commencing with Borneo and other Malayan islands in the tropics of the southern hemisphere, and proceeding north, we find them recorded in the mountain regions of all the intervening countries that have been botanically investigated, even to northern and extreme arctic Siberia. As we proceed westward into Europe, they gradually disappear, one only inhabiting Sweden and Norway (*R. Lapponicum*), and that seems not to extend to the western coasts.

In the vast continent of North America, the cool hilly grounds, with moisture, of the middle and southern states, yield only *R. maximum* (which, however, is found also in Canada), *R. macrophyllum*, Don, confined to the west side of the Rocky Mountains, *R. Catawbiense* and *R. punctatum*, which two have a very limited range. The anomalous *R. albiflorum*, with white flowers and deciduous leaves, is only seen in the Rocky Mountains, about lat. 52°. As might be expected, in the alpine and arctic regions the northern European kinds appear; for example, *R. Lapponicum* has been detected on the White Mountains, Massachusetts, on the summit of Mount Mary, Essex County, New York, at an elevation of 5,400 feet on the Rocky Mountains, in Labrador, and along the coasts of the Polar Sea; while in Behring's Straits, the *R. Kamschaticum* again appears. No species grows in Mexico or near the coasts of Oregon or California, and none in the isthmus of Panama. Throughout the whole of Africa[1] and Australia, the genus is unknown; and it will be observed that it only enters the southern hemisphere through the medium of the Indian Archipelago.

When it is borne in mind that, as above stated, Mr. Griffith, in an excursion to one mountain in Bootan, detected eight species,[2] and that the author of the present work, during a very limited sojourn in Sikkim, and with little means of prosecuting extensive researches, owing to the nature of the country and the hostile feeling entertained towards the English by the Rajah, yet collected and described eleven species, of which nine were new, it may, I think, be fairly conceded that if the maximum of Rhododendrons be in Asia, their head-quarters are on the lofty ranges of the Eastern Himalaya, where the mild and moist atmosphere is eminently suited to their habit.—Ed.

[1] Boissier, indeed, in his *Voyage Botanique en Espagne*, says of the *R. Ponticum*:—"Hab. verosimiliter in Atlante,"—but I know not upon what authority.

[2] How far these species may accord with those of Sikkim, or whether any will do so, cannot be determined, until the Hon. the E. I. C. shall be pleased to unlock the treasures contributed by Mr. Griffith to the Herbarium stores in the possession of the Company; and there is now happily a prospect of this long-wished-for event taking place. The few Rhododendrons that have been edited by Dr. Wight we know to be very different and of peculiar interest.

THE

RHODODENDRONS

OF

SIKKIM-HIMALAYA.

IT has been well remarked by the illustrious Wallich, (the Father of Nepalese Botany,) that in Nepal the genus *Rhododendron* claims the highest rank amongst the plants of that rich kingdom. From the proximity of Sikkim to Nepal, a similarity in the botanical features of these countries might be expected; and also that the difference should rather exist in individual species than in the genera or higher groups. The outline of the two countries is very similar, their latitude the same, so is their geology, and the difference in climate is slight, and only evident in the increased humidity of the eastern region.

Rhododendrons are distributed in Sikkim as they are in Nepal, crowning those sub-Himalayan hills which attain 7,000 feet of elevation, and at a still greater altitude increasing in number of species and individuals: some species being replaced by others which have no greater, perhaps less, apparent adaptation for resisting vicissitudes of climate, and yet accompanying several of the more local kinds throughout the elevations they severally attain.

I. As is frequently the case with large genera, one or more species, distinguished by peculiarity of distribution, often present some anomalies in botanical or other characters, whether in the unusual habit, mode of growth, or singular outline, colour, or more important feature. So it is with the Sikkim *Rhododendrons*. *R. Dalhousiæ*, the only one found so low as at 7,000 feet, and thence upwards for 3,000 feet more, differs from all its congeners of Northern India in its epiphytal mode of growth,[1] its sweet-scented flowers, slender habit, whorled branches, and in the length of time during which it continues in bloom. It is much the largest-flowered species with which I am acquainted, and has more membranous leaves than any of the others. With all these striking anomalies, it does not, however, present one character of calyx, corolla, stamens, or pistil, entitling it to separation from the genus. In possessing a large foliaceous

[1] In Sikkim, *Vaccinium* offers a parallel case. The *V. serpens* (?), an epiphyte on very large trees, inhabits a much lower level and ranges through many more feet in elevation than any of its congeners. [In Borneo it will be remembered that Mr. Low discovered epiphytal Rhododendrons; and Mr. William Lobb, several in Java. Ed.]

C

calyx, it is one of the most perfect plants of the whole, and in its characters of flower and fruit is far more closely allied to the typical or scarlet-flowered group, than is the section to which the following belongs.

II. *Rhododendron Falconeri*, a white-flowered species, is eminently characteristic of the genus in habit, place of growth, and locality, never occurring below 10,000 feet. On the other hand it is peculiar in its ten-lobed corolla, numerous stamens, and many-celled ovary, superb foliage and many-flowered capitula. This multiplication of parts and development of foliage and trunk give it a striking appearance; but there is an almost total absence of calyx, an organ sufficiently evident in other species. It is allied to a species discovered by the lamented Griffith in Bootan, the *R. grande*, Wight, published in the Calcutta Journ. Nat. Hist. vol. viii. p. 176, [and since in Dr. Wight's Icones, vol. iv. p. 6. t. 1202].[1]

III. A third white-flowered group contains but one Sikkim species, the *R. argenteum*, a very conspicuous tree at an elevation of between 8,000 and 9,000 feet. In beauty of foliage it nearly equals the last mentioned (*R. Falconeri*), and the flowers are larger than in any but *R. Dalhousiæ*, and of the same form as those of the scarlet group; the stamens are of the normal number, but the ovarium is many-celled. Though evidently distinct, this species combines the characters of most of the other groups. In size of flower and colour, as already observed, it resembles *R. Dalhousiæ*, as it does in its unusually membranous leaves;[2] in the colour of the flower, size of foliage, small calyx, and many-celled ovarium, *R. Falconeri*;—while the number of stamens, general habit, silvery under-surface of leaf, &c., connect it with *R. arboreum*.[3]

IV. A singular set includes the dwarfish kinds to which *R. cinnabarinum* and *R. Roylii* belong. The flowers are small, the corolla is subcoriaceous, narrowed at the base of the tube, and its colour is a peculiarly dirty brick-red, somewhat iridescent with blue in bud, and its lobes are rounded, subacute, not notched or wrinkled. The calyces are small, coriaceous, and squamous in both; in one the lobes are remarkably unequal. In the number of stamens, cells of the ovarium, &c., they agree with the usual characters of the genus.

V. Of the normal or typical group, indicated to be such by the number of species it contains, by the prevalence of scarlet flowers, uniformity of corolla and number of parts, there are two subdivisions: one has a fully developed calyx, in the other the calyx is very small and coriaceous. *R. lancifolium* and *R. barbatum* represent the former section, in both of which that organ is as conspicuous as in *R. Dalhousiæ*. *R. arboreum*, *R. Wallichii*, and *R. Campbelliæ*, belong to the latter section. The species of this group known to me are all trees, of contracted range and gay flowers.

VI. The little *R. elæagnoides* may be classed in another group: it is a very alpine plant, of which I possess only the foliage and fruit. Its scaliness (a character which seems most conspicuous in the smaller and more alpine species) allies it to *R. cinnabarinum*, but it is apparently single-flowered and calyculate.

The sub-Himalayan mountains are surely the *centrum* of this truly fine genus, distinguished by the number and variety of its species and groups, by the great size and eminent beauty of several, which form conspicuous features in the landscape over many degrees of longitude, through a great variety of elevations, and clothe a vast amount of surface.

[1] From this figure and description it will be seen, that although in many respects near *R. Falconeri*, especially in the dense many-flowered capitulum, smallish many-cleft corolla, numerous stamens and cells of the ovary, yet that it is quite distinct in the smaller cuspidate leaves, white and scaly beneath, and in the deeply ten-lobed corolla. Ed.

[2] The term *membranous* is of course used comparatively here; in no species is the foliage truly so,—*less coriaceous* were the better, though more cumbrous, term.

[3] Dr. Hooker had here stated of *R. argenteum*, that *R. Griffithianum*, Wight, in Calcutta Journal of Natural History, vol. viii. p. 176, is probably a close ally of this; but that has since been published in Dr. Wight's Icones Plant. Indiae Orientalis, vol. iv. p. 6. t. 1201, and proves to belong to, or rather to constitute, a very distant section, having very lax racemose flowers, a nearly entire, spreading, scutelliform calyx (quite unlike that of any other species), many (15?) stamens, and ten cells to the ovary. It is a native of Bootan. Ed.

The Neelgherries, Ceylon, and the Malay Archipelago contain, each, some species which prove the affinity of their Floras to that of the Himalaya. The same is the case with the great mountains of Northern Asia, Central, Southern, and, especially, Eastern Europe, the Ural, and Pontus. The genus extends even to the Polar regions, diminishing in the size of the species and number as we recede from the Himalaya: in North America they appear again, though under a very different aspect from that they present on the subtropical mountains of Asia.

Wide though this distinction is, it is far from uniform, the Himalaya itself offering most remarkable anomalies. My friend Dr. Thomson (now engaged in a botanical mission to Thibet) informs me that the genus is not found in Cashmere; nor, during all the wanderings of that intrepid and indefatigable naturalist in the Trans-Sutledge Himalaya and Thibet, has he met with one representative of it. He detected, indeed, in the country south of the Chenaub, both the *R. arboreum* and *R. campanulatum*, and which is probably their western limit.

In North-west India, the genus *Rhododendron* is first seen on the Kunawur hills, and advancing east, follows the sub-Himalayan range for its whole length, the species increasing in number as far as Sikkim and Bootan; thence the genus is continued to the Mishmee hills, the eastern extremity of the range, crossing the Brahmaputra to that lofty range which divides the water-shed of the Irawaddi from that of the Brahmaputra.

Though scarcely found, throughout this long line of upwards of 1,200 miles, below 4,000 feet, the Rhododendrons still affect a warm and damp climate, where the winters are mild. The English naturalist, who is only familiar with the comparatively small hardy American and European species, would scarcely expect this. A certain degree of winter-cold and perpetual humidity is necessary; but the summer-heat is quite tropical where some of the genus prevail, and snow rarely falls and never rests on several of those peculiar to Sikkim.

R. arboreum, according to Captain Madden, inhabits various localities between 3,000 and 10,000 feet: this is in Kamaoon, where, of course, the genus would descend lowest; and the range is incomparably greater than that of any other species, at least of those found in Sikkim.[4] Dr. Griffith, after extended wanderings in Bootan, gives the limits of the genus in that country as between 4,292 and 12,478 feet, which is a lower level by 3,000 feet than they are known to descend to in Sikkim. In the extreme east of Assam, where the Himalaya itself diverges or sends lofty spurs to stem the Brahmaputra, on the Phien Pass to Ava, Rhododendrons ascend from 5,400 to 12,000 feet, to the upper limit of arboreous vegetation, and perhaps still higher.

During my limited excursions in Sikkim, I gathered eleven species (and I believe that more exist), a greater number than Griffith obtained in Bootan; so that I cannot but regard this longitude as the head-quarters of the genus in the Himalaya, and that chain as the especial region of the genus in the Old World. Here too I may remark (as is the case with the *Coniferæ* of Tasmania and *Cacteæ* of Mexico), the species are most limited in habitat, where, numerically, the genus is the largest, the *R. arboreum*, however, having a much wider range than any other species found in Sikkim.

[4] Dr. Hooker had here inserted "where *R. arboreum* is unknown," that is, in Sikkim. But one of his own excellent figures, sent home as representing a new species, is, I have no hesitation in saying, the true *R. arboreum*, coinciding entirely with the original figure of Sir James E. Smith (Exotic Botany, Tab. 6), and with original specimens given me by the same distinguished botanist and existing in my own Herbarium. Nor need we be surprised that Dr. Hooker should have fallen into this error, with few books and no authentic specimens to consult; especially when it is borne in mind that his eye had been accustomed to the plants that pass under that name in our gardens, but which have been so hybridized by cultivators, either to increase their beauty or with the intention of rendering the offspring more hardy, that an original plant or tree of *Rhododendron arboreum* is almost as rare in England as is the normal single-flowered state of the *Corchorus* (*Kerria*) *Japonica*. Let it be further observed that other distinguished Botanists have confounded distinct species with the *R. arboreum*: I allude especially to the plant so called by Dr. Wight of the Neelgherries (Icones Plant. Ind. Orient. tab. 1201), which is the *R. Nilagiricum* of Zenker (Plant. Nilag. cum Ic., and of Bot. Mag. tab. 4381). No one who compares native specimens of these two plants can have any hesitation in pronouncing them distinct. Ed.

Westward again, as far, indeed, as the western termination of the Himalaya, the species descend lower than in Bootan: an anomalous fact, for which, in our ignorance of the contrasting features which may distinguish the Eastern from the Central Himalaya, I can only assign conjectural causes. Among these may be the proximity of the ocean to the Sikkim portion of the range, and the presence of heavy mountain-masses covered with winter, and even perpetual, snow, to the south and east of the upper extremity of the Brahmaputra, whereas the genus is found nearly 2,000 feet lower than in Sikkim. The descent of the snow line in Upper Assam to 14,000 or 15,000 feet, is no doubt due to the same causes, and this is a most remarkable fact. Uniformity of temperature, excessive humidity, and a broken surface, produce the same effect here as in the high southern and antarctic latitudes,—favouring the formation of snow and its permanence, and also extending the range of tropical forms upwards to a greater elevation, and the descent of temperate or arctic forms to a lower one; of which no stronger proof can be required than the descent of *Rosaceæ* and *Ericeæ*, and the great elevation which *Rafflesia*, *Balanophora*, and other eminently tropical genera, attain on the Himalaya.

Too much stress cannot be laid upon this fact, that the snow-line ascends with the latitude on the Himalaya, from 14,500 feet at its south-east extreme in Upper Assam, south of the Brahmaputra, lat. 27° N., to 20,000 feet at its north-west extreme in the regions near and beyond the Sutledge, in lat. 36° and 37° N. Had the level of perpetual snow remained uniform throughout these 600 miles of northing, then climate would have only annihilated the effect of distance from the equator. But if we allow that, *cæteris paribus*, a degree of latitude is the index of a change of 300 feet in the snow-line, we must also allow that the limit of perpetual snow is 8,000 feet lower in Upper Assam than its height on the Sutledge Himalaya would indicate, being 15,000 instead of 23,000 feet; and, *vice versâ*, that if 14,500 is that limit at Assam, as determined by latitude alone, in Kunawur we should have it at 11,000 instead of 20,000.

Only four species, *R. Dalhousiæ*, *R. Campbelliæ*, *R. argenteum*, and *R. arboreum* grow near Darjeeling. The second and fourth form scattered bushes at 7,500 and 8,000 feet: the *R. argenteum* is a small tree, at 8,000 and 9,000 feet, strangely associated with *Balanophora*, *Convallaria*, *Paris*, *Sphæropteris*, *Laurus*, and *Magnolia*.

It was on the ascent of Tonglo, a mountain on the Nepalese frontier, that I beheld the Rhododendrons in all their magnificence and luxuriance. At 7,000 feet, where the woods were still dense and subtropical, mingling with Ferns, *Pothos*, Peppers, and Figs, the ground was strewed with the large lily-like flowers of *R. Dalhousiæ*, dropping from the epiphytal plants on the enormous Oaks overhead, and mixed with the egg-like flowers of a new Magnoliaceous tree, which fall before expanding and diffuse a powerful aromatic odour, more strong, but far less sweet, than that of the *Rhododendron*. So conspicuous were these two blossoms, that my rude guides called out, "Here are lilies and eggs, Sir, growing out of the ground!"—No bad comparison. Passing the region of Tree-Ferns, Wallnut, and Chestnut, yet still in that of the Alder, Birch, large-leaved Oak (whose leaves are often eighteen inches long), we enter that of the broad-spathed *Arum* (which raises a crested head like that of the Cobra de capel), the *Kadsura*, *Stauntonia*, *Convallaria*, and many *Rosaceæ*. The paths here are much steeper, carried along narrow ridges or over broken masses of rock, which are scaled by the aid of interwoven roots of trees. On these rocks grow *Hymenophylla*, a few *Orchideæ*, *Begonia*, *Cyrtandraceæ*, *Aroideæ* of curious forms, the anomalous genus *Streptolirion* of Edgeworth, and various *Cryptogamiæ*, and the *Rhododendron arboreum* is first met with, its branches often loaded with pendulous mosses and lichens, especially *Usnea* and *Borrera*. Along the flat ridges, towards the top, the Yew appears with scattered trees of *Rhododendron argenteum*, succeeded by *R. Campbelliæ*. At the very summit, the majority of the wood consists of this last species, amongst which and next in abundance occurs the *R. barbatum*, with here and there, especially on the eastern slopes, *R. Falconeri*.

Mingled with these are *Pyri*, *Pruni*, Maples, Barberries, and Azaleas, *Olea*, *Ilex*, *Limonia*, *Hydrangea*, several *Caprifoliaceæ*, *Gaultheria*, and *Andromeda*; the Apple and the Rose are most abundant. *Stauntonia*, with its glorious racemes of purple flowers, creeps over all; so do *Kadsura* and *Ochna*; whilst a Currant, with erect racemes, grows epiphytally on *Rhododendron* and on *Pyrus*.

The habits of the species of *Rhododendron* differ considerably, and, confined as I was to one favourable spot by a deluge of rain, I had ample time to observe four of them. *R. Campbelliæ*, the only one in full flower early in May, is the most prevalent, the ropes of my tent spanning an area between three of them. Some were a mass of scarlet blossom, displaying a sylvan scene of the most gorgeous description. Mr. Nightingale's[1] Rhododendron groves, I thought, may surpass these in form and luxuriance of foliage, or in outline of individual specimens; but for splendour of colour those of the Himalaya can only be compared with the *Butea frondosa* of the plains. Many of their trunks spread from the centre thirty or forty feet every way, and together form a hemispherical mass, often forty yards across and from twenty to fifty feet in height! The stems and branches of these aged trees, gnarled and rugged, the bark dark-coloured and clothed with

[1] At Embley near Romsey, Hants, the seat of William Edward Nightingale, Esq., whose beautiful grounds boast of drives through what may really be called woods or groves of Rhododendrons, many of them self-sown.—The mention of these grounds (adorned with exotic Rhododendrons) by a naturalist luxuriating amidst the aboriginal species of the lofty mountains of Sikkim-Himalaya, makes me desirous to introduce here a brief notice of the plants in question. I could not trust my own memory for a correct statement of what it has been my privilege to see, but Miss Nightingale has obligingly communicated to me the following particulars:—

"Our Rhododendrons were chiefly planted about thirty years ago: the largest number are in an exceedingly wet 'bottom' of deep black peat full of drains, sheltered with sloping banks of Birch and Fir, with a good deal of Laurel, large Kalmias and Azaleas near the road. This part was originally a nursery-garden of about four acres: the shrubs have been cut continually to keep the road clear, and now make a bank seventeen or eighteen feet high. They are scattered over the high ground (a dry black sand) for about two miles, where they cover another bank of heathery soil and another bottom of the deep peat. There are not above a dozen of the *R. maximum* amongst them, and about three times as many of the *arboreum* and hybrid Scarlets which we find quite hardy, but which seem to flower best in the high and dry situations. The *Ponticum* and var. *roseum* seed themselves to a great extent, and the consequence is an immense variety in the shape, size, and colour of the flowers, hardly any two plants being quite alike.

"The largest single Rhododendron is one hundred and fifty feet round and twenty feet high: there are several of ninety-seven and ninety-eight feet round, but these have been cramped for room by their neighbours. The tallest I can find grows between a Birch and a Portugal Laurel, and is twenty-five feet high, its single upright stem measuring nineteen inches in circumference. It is quite an exception, for they fork generally immediately on emerging from the ground; and though there is one which measures five feet ten inches in the girth of its trunk an inch from the ground, yet as he leaves his good ways and divides immediately after, I am not sure you will grant him his diploma as a tree. The forks are from eighteen inches to two feet in circumference. The variegated kind, with long footstalks to the flowers, has perhaps the thickest stem with us. The outside branches of the large individuals root themselves all round and make impenetrable thickets. We plant out the seedlings, which come up very thickly wherever an open space gives them room, and they are now scattered over most of the wild ground about.

"I think this is pretty nearly all we have to tell, but we may add that the Kalmias and Yellow Azaleas are some of them ten feet high and wide in proportion."

It may be interesting to record some particulars of another favoured spot for Rhododendrons, namely, Penllergare, Glamorgan, the seat of Dillwyn Llewellyn, Esq., who writes in reply to my queries:—

"The soil and climate of this district suit that class of plants well, as is attested by the seedlings of the common *Rhododendron Ponticum*, which appear in thousands throughout our woods. The rough sketch I enclose is of this species: it measures in height fifteen feet ten inches, and completely covers a circumference of one hundred and ten feet. The plant grows by itself upon a lawn, without any trees to overshadow or interfere with it, and it forms a perfectly symmetrical and compact shrub, with dense foliage and short-jointed wood.

"We have also a specimen of *R. arboreum*, var. *roseum*, nine feet four inches in height, and in circumference forty-eight feet: it was planted fifteen years ago and has never received the slightest protection. Like the last, it stands alone on a lawn, and is of a beautifully compact form. It has 3,200 flower-buds now upon it. The single stem from which it rises measures one foot nine inches in girth.

"The American species also flourish here with great vigour. A specimen of *R. Catawbiense* measures nine feet six inches in height, and covers forty-one feet six inches of circumference: this, however, is much younger than either of the preceding. It is also growing under the shade of large oak-trees, for which reason it is somewhat drawn and not so fine and thick in its growth as it might otherwise have been."

It may be observed that Mr. Loudon, in his Arboretum Britannicum, has not described any specimens of *Rhododendron arboreum* of the size above given. The largest he has noticed are at Wimbledon House, thirty-three feet in the spread of its branches; at Cuffnells in Hampshire, thirty-nine feet ditto; Woburn Abbey, twenty-eight feet ditto; Shipley Hall, Derbyshire, fifty-six feet ditto, and sixteen feet the greatest height. Ed.

D

spongy moss, often bend down and touch the ground: the foliage, moreover, is scanty, dark green, and far from graceful; so that notwithstanding the gorgeous colouring of the blossoms, the trees when out of flower, like the *Fuchsias* of Cape Horn, are the gloomy denizens of a most gloomy region. *R. Campbelliæ* and *R. barbatum* I observed to fringe a little swampy tarn on the summit of the mountain,—a peculiarly chilly-looking, small lake, bordered with *Sphagnum*, and half-choked with *Carices* and other sedges: the atmosphere was loaded with mist, and the place seems as if it would be aguish if it could, but was checked by the cold climate. *R. barbatum* had almost passed its flowering season: it is a less abundant and smaller tree than the last mentioned, but more beautiful in the brighter green and denser foliage, clean, papery, light-coloured bark, the whole forming a more picturesque mass.

Along the north-east and exposed ridges only, grew the *R. Falconeri*, in foliage incomparably the finest. It throws out one or two trunks, clean and smooth, thirty feet or so high, sparingly branched: the branches terminated by the immense leaves, deep green above, edged with yellow, and rusty red-brown below. The flowers are smaller, but more numerous in each head than in the two last mentioned (*R. Campbelliæ* and *R. barbatum*).

The temperature of the earth in which the above species grew, was, in the middle of May, at twenty-seven inches below the surface where the roots are chiefly developed, 49° 5′ at all hours of the day: that of the air varied from 50° to 60°.

In naming the new species before me of this eminently Himalayan genus, I have wished to record the services of some of those gentlemen who, besides Mr. Griffith (to whom a species had been already dedicated by Dr. Wight), have most deeply studied the vegetable productions of the country: they are Drs. Wallich, Royle, and Falconer. With their names that of Dr. Campbell, the Political Resident at Darjeeling, author of various excellent Essays on the Agriculture, Arts, Products, and People, &c., of Nepal and Sikkim, is no less appropriately associated; and in compliment to his amiable Lady I designate that Rhododendron which is most characteristic of Darjeeling vegetation; while to the Lady of the present Governor-General of India, I have, as a mark of grateful esteem and respect, dedicated the noblest species of the whole race. *J. D. H.*

Tab. II

J.D.H. del. Fitch, lith.

Reeve, Benham & Reeve, Imp.

RHODODENDRON DALHOUSIÆ, Hook. fil.

1.

RHODODENDRON DALHOUSIÆ, *Hook. fil.*

Lady Dalhousie's Rhododendron.

TAB. I., II.

Frutex gracilis, ramis remotis verticillatis vage patentibus, foliis obovato-ellipticis obtusis coriaceo-membranaceis subter pallidioribus sparse rufo-punctatis, basi in petiolum attenuatis, floribus (amplis albis) 3–7 capitato-umbellatis, lobis calycinis foliaceis oblongis obtusis, corolla campanulata basi profunde 5-foveolata, staminibus 10 filamentis inferne pilosis, ovario 5-loculari.

HAB. Parasitical on the trunks of large trees, especially Oaks and Magnolias. Sikkim-Himalaya: elevation 7,000–9,500 feet. *Fl.* April to July.

A straggling *shrub*, six to eight feet high, always seen growing, like the tropical *Orchideæ*, among moss and Ferns and *Aroideæ*, upon the trunks of large trees: the *stems* clothed with a reddish papery bark, the *branches* straggling, patent, whorled, the whorls distant; each branch bearing its leaves and flowers only at the extremity. *Leaves* few, patent or reflexed, petiolate, about four inches and a half to five in length, elliptical-obovate, between coriaceous and membranaceous, obtuse at the base, attenuated below into a more or less downy *footstalk*, about half an inch long, the margin plane (not revolute), the upper surface darkish-green, inclining to a yellow hue, even on the surface, beneath paler, dotted with very minute, scattered, rusty-coloured scales or points (scarcely sufficient to change the general tint), the mid-rib prominent, the rather close parallel *nerves* scarcely so. *Flowers* three to seven in a terminal, umbellate *head*, the spread of which is greater than that of the leaves. *Peduncles* nearly an inch long, stout, cylindrical, downy. *Bracteas* ligulate, membranaceous. *Calyx* large, deeply divided almost to the base into five ovato-elliptical, very obtuse, spreading, foliaceous lobes. *Corolla* very large, three inches and a half to four inches and a half long, and as broad at the mouth, campanulate, white, with an occasional tinge of rose, in size and colour and general shape almost resembling that of the white Bourbon Lily, *Lilium candidum*, very fragrant. At the contracted base of the tube are five deep foveolæ. *Lobes* of the *limb* nearly equal, very broad, rounded, waved, spreading. *Stamens* ten: *filaments* longer than the tube, curved upwards, downy below. *Anther* oblong-ovate, dark purple-brown. *Ovary* ovate, furfuraceous, five-celled, tapering into the thickened *style*, which is longer than the stamens. *Stigma* an orbicular, convex disk.

Certainly, whether we regard the size, the colour, or the fragrance of the blossoms of this plant, they are the noblest of the genus *Rhododendron*. The odour partakes of that of the Lemon. In age the flowers assume a delicate roseate tinge and sometimes become spotted with orange, which rather adds to, than detracts from, their beauty.

TAB. I. Represents a plant of *R. Dalhousiæ*, on a very reduced scale, in its native locality.

TAB. II. Flowering branch. 1. Stamen. 2. Anther. 3. Pistil:—*natural size*. 4. Section of ovary. 5. Pollen with boyau:—*magnified*.

Tab. III.

J.D.H. del. Fitch, lith. Reeve, Benham & Reeve, imp.

RHODODENDRON BARBATUM, Wall.

2.

RHODODENDRON BARBATUM, *Wall.*

Bristly Rhododendron.

TAB. III.

Arboreum, foliis elliptico-lanceolatis acutis basi obtusis coriaceis marginibus subrecurvis utrinque glaberrimis subtus pallidioribus supra impresse venosis, petiolo tuberculoso longe ramulisque glanduloso-setosis, bracteis alabastrisque viscidis, floribus dense capitatis mediocribus sanguineis, lobis calycinis foliaceis viscidis ovato-ellipticis appressis, staminibus 10, filamentis glabris, ovarii glanduloso-hirsuti loculis 5–8.

RHODODENDRON barbatum. *Wall. Cat.* no. 757. *Don, Syst. Gard. and Bot.* vol. iii. p. 844. *De Cand. Prodr.* vol. vii. p. 721. *Hook. in Bot. Mag.* sub Tab. 4381; *in Gard. Chron.* 1848 (with a wood-cut).

HAB. Gossain Than, *Wallich.* Summit of Tonglo, in Sikkim-Himalaya, alt. 10,000 feet. *Fl.* April.

A *tree,* from forty to sixty feet high, branched from the base. Main *trunks* few, inclined, compressed, clothed with reddish, papyraceous *bark,* destitute of Lichens and Mosses. *Branches* numerous, floriferous at their apices. *Leaves,* in the very young state, sparingly hairy and ciliated; when fully developed, five to seven inches long, and from one and a half to two inches and more wide, elliptical-lanceolate, acute, rather broader above the middle, the margins reflexed and rough to the touch from the presence of minute harsh ciliæ, penninerved; the *nerves* sunk on the upper surface, and there dull but full green, paler and quite glabrous beneath and destitute of scales or down of every kind, but turning to an ochraceous tint when dry. *Petioles* short, (half an inch) thick, somewhat tubercled and beset with long, rigid, black *setæ* or hairs, glanduliferous at the point: these hairs or bristles often extend a little way up the mid-rib beneath. *Flowers* moderately sized, of a deep puce or blood-colour, collected into a compact, globose *head,* four to five inches in diameter. *Bracteas* oblong or ovate, the inner ones silky, all more or less glutinous. *Calyx* large, scarcely silky, deeply cut into five, erect, large, foliaceous ovate *lobes,* half an inch long. *Filaments* ten, glabrous. *Anthers* short, and, as well as the nearly straight *style,* included. *Ovary* oblong, clothed with glandular hairs. *Stigma* small, obtuse. *Fruit* setose, rich brown, included in the persistent calyx.

One of the most beautiful of the Himalayan species, and readily distinguished by the bristly petioles and young branches. [Although in cultivation in England, at least in the Upton Nursery, Chester, of Messrs. Dickson, no coloured figure has yet been published. The present one will serve to show what a treasure is in store for our open borders, seeing that it has proved perfectly hardy in the Nursery above mentioned. ED.]

TAB. III. *Rhododendron barbatum,* Wall.; flowering branch. 1. Flower and bract:—*natural size.* 2. Stamen. 3. Pistil. 4. Section of ovary:—*magnified.* 5. Capsule:—*natural size.*

Tab. IV.

J. D. H. del. Fitch lith.

Reeve Benham & Reeve imp.

RHODODENDRON LANCIFOLIUM, Hook. fil.

Tab. V.

J. D. H. del. Fitch lith.

RHODODENDRON WALLICHII, Hook. fil.

4.

RHODODENDRON WALLICHII, *Hook. fil.*

Dr. Wallich's Rhododendron.

TAB. V.

Frutescens, foliis coriaceis ellipticis acutis basi cordatis supra lævissimis petiolisque glaberrimis marginibus revolutis subtus pallidis costam versus punctis ferrugineis pulverulento-tomentosis, floribus 6–8 capitato-racemosis, calycibus lobis brevissimis coriaceis subacutis, ovarii glaberrimi loculis 5.

HAB. Interior of Sikkim-Himalaya.

A *shrub*, attaining a height of from eight to ten feet, with the *branches* rugged, rather tortuous, clothed with dark brown bark. *Leaves* mostly confined to the apex of the ultimate branches, three or four inches long, of a remarkably neat appearance, almost exactly elliptical, coriaceous, full green, very even, most indistinctly nerved, glabrous above, as is the somewhat wrinkled *petiole*, the base cordate, the margins recurved, the apex suddenly acute, the underside pale green, very obsoletely nerved, and quite glabrous, except towards the costa, where it is dotted as it were with dark, ferruginous, pulverulent tomentum. *Flowers* large, handsome, six to eight in a capitate *raceme*. *Pedicels* less than an inch long, glabrous. *Bracteas* deciduous, exterior ones glabrous, viscid, or sparingly downy. *Calyx* very short and small, the *lobes* triangular, rather obtuse, glabrous. *Corolla* lilac-colour; the *tube* campanulate, the *limb* spreading, of five nearly equal, rounded *lobes*, the upper one however the largest, all two-lobed, sprinkled with deeper rose-coloured dots within. *Stamens* ten, as long as the tube. *Filaments* white. *Anthers* purple-brown. *Style* filiform, longer than the stamens. *Ovary* glabrous, oblong-ovate, five-lobed, five-celled.

A very distinct and handsome species, worthy to bear the name of one who may justly be called "Botanicorum Indicorum facile princeps." Its leaves are quite unlike any Indian species, and the flowers in colour and size resemble those of the much cultivated *R. Ponticum*.

TAB. V. *Rhododendron Wallichii.* Fig. 1. Stamen. 2. Calyx and pistil. 3. Calyx and section of the ovary;—*magnified.*

Tab. VI.

J. D. H. del. Fitch lith.

RHODODENDRON CAMPBELLIÆ, Hook.fil.

5.

RHODODENDRON CAMPBELLIÆ, *Hook. fil.*

Mrs. Campbell's Rhododendron.

TAB. VI.

Arboreum, foliis coriaceis oblongo-lanceolatis acuminatis basi cordatis supra glaberrimis subtus rufo- v.-ferrugineo- tomentosis marginibus recurvis, petiolis pedunculis calyceque furfuraceis, capitulis densifloris, calycis parvi lobis brevissimis, corollæ puniceæ intus maculatæ lobis 4 rotundatis integris unico (superiore) bilobo, staminibus 10, ovario pubescente 7–10 loculari.

HAB. Sikkim-Himalaya, frequent: alt. 9,000–10,000 feet. *Fl.* April and May.

This may be called a *tree*, attaining, as it does not unfrequently, a height of forty feet, detected in various localities, at the elevation just mentioned above the level of the sea. On the summit of Tonglo it is the prevailing plant, and there, when in full flower, it exhibits a truly magnificent spectacle, gorgeous with scarlet heads of blossoms. So far as I could observe, the greater the elevation above the sea at which this species grows, the redder or more deeply ferruginous was the under-side of the leaf. This ferruginous tomentum, together with the obtuse and cordate base of the leaf, are the characters which distinguish it from *R. arboreum*, as the very different outline of the leaves does from *R. Nilagiricum*. *R. cinnamomeum*, Wall. (*R. arboreum*, var. of Lindley and De Candolle) differs in the white (perhaps not the normal) colour of the flowers, and in the two-lobed segments of all the lobes of the corolla. In the present species the peduncles, styles, and base of the filaments are red.

TAB. VI. *Rhododendron Campbelliæ.* Fig. 1. Calyx and pistil. 2. Section of ovary. 3. Stamen :—*magnified.*

6.

RHODODENDRON ARBOREUM, *Sm.*

Scarlet arborescent Rhododendron.

Subarboreum, foliis coriaceis lanceolatis subacuminatis basi in petiolum attenuatis supra glabris subtus argenteis marginibus subrecurvis, capitulis densifloris, bracteis sericeis, calycis parvi lobis brevissimis, corolla punicea fauce supra tuboque intus purpureo-maculatis, staminibus 10, ovario sericeo 8–10-loculari.

RHODODENDRON arboreum. *Smith, Ex. Bot.* p. 9. t. 6. *Lindl. in Bot. Reg.* t. 890. *Hook. Ex. Fl.* t. 168. *Don, Fl. Nep.* p. 154.

RHODODENDRON puniceum. *Roxb. Fl. Ind.* vol. ii. p. 409.

BOORANS. "*Hardw. in Trans. Asiat. Soc.* vol. vi. p. 359."

HAB. Darjeeling, and along the Himalaya, extending east, we believe, according to Mr. Griffith's notes, into Bootan, and west as far as the valley of the Chenaub, in long. 77°. (*T. Thomson.*)

[We need not occupy our space with any description of this species. An excellent drawing of it, sent by Dr. Hooker as a new species from Darjeeling, proves to be the true *R. arboreum*, the first, indeed, of the Indian *Rhododendrons* that was discovered. We can refer with confidence to the synonyms above-quoted, which is more than can be said of many that bear this name. The figure in English Botany, however, does not exhibit the under-side of the leaf; and the purplish spots or dots are omitted by the Indian artist, from whose drawing the plate was copied. Dr. Lindley's figure is very characteristic; but that by Dr. Greville, in the Exotic Flora, is particularly faithful. The distinguishing marks of this species are the almost exactly lanceolate leaves, more or less acuminated, tapering at the base into the footstalk, and clothed beneath with a compact silvery film, neither to be called silvery nor downy. ED.]

J. D. H. del. Fitch lith.

Reeve Benham & Reeve imp.

RHODODENDRON ROYLII, Hook. fil.

7.

RHODODENDRON ROYLII, *Hook. fil.*

Dr. Royle's Rhododendron.

TAB. VII.

Arbuscula, foliis coriaceis ellipticis acuminulatis margine revolutis basi obtusis subcordatis supra glaberrimis nitidis subtus ochraceo-fuscis pulverulentis, petiolis transversim rugosis, capitulis 6–8-floris, lobis (pedunculisque resinoso-glandulosis) brevissimis rotundatis, corollæ intus lineatæ segmentis rotundatis acutis, staminibus 10, ovarii puberuli loculis 5.

HAB. Sikkim-Himalaya; mountains of the interior. *Fl.* April and May.

This and the following species (*R. cinnabarinum*) belong to a group distinguished by the small size of the plants, the brownish-red colour of the corolla, and its nearly equal and sharp segments. As species they are all easily recognised. The present is a *shrub*, with almost exactly oval or elliptical leaves, clothed beneath with an ochraceous-brown pulverulent substance. *Petioles* obscurely winged. *Flowers* in a lax *head*, from four or five to eight. *Corolla* subcoriaceous, small, with campanulate tube, striated within, limb not much spreading, the five lobes rounded, but coming to an acute point, the points tipped with bluish-green. In its unexpanded state, the corolla is tinged with blue. *Peduncles* slender, short, warted as it were. *Filaments* slightly ciliated at the base. *Ovary* short. *Style* and *stigma* green.

TAB. VII. *Rhododendron Roylii.* Fig. 1. Stamen. 2. Calyx and pistil. 3. Section of ovary:—*magnified.*

Tab. VIII.

J. D. H. del. Fitch, lith.

Reeve, Benham & Reeve, imp.

RHODODENDRON CINNABARINUM, Hook. fil.

8.

RHODODENDRON CINNABARINUM, *Hook. fil.*

Cinnabar-leaved Rhododendron.

Tab. VIII.

Frutex, ramis gracilibus tortuosis, foliis ovato-lanceolatis acutis marginibus subrevolutis basi in petiolum tuberculosum attenuatis glabris, supra copiose reticulatim venosis subtus pallidis rufisve squamuloso-punctatis, floribus parvis capitatis cinnabarinis, lobis calycinis linearibus inæqualibus pedunculisque grosse glanduloso-squamosis, corollæ infundibuliformis lobis omnibus rotundatis acutis, staminibus 10, filamentis basi pilosis, ovario 5-loculari furfuraceo.

Hab. Sub-Himalaya mountains, interior of Sikkim. *Fl.* April and May.

A small *shrub*. *Leaves* two to three inches long, an inch wide, slightly tapering at both extremities, glabrous, beautifully and closely reticulated above, beneath often reddish, punctato-squamulose : the *costa* terminating in a short produced point. *Petiole* glabrous, wrinkled. *Peduncles* short, clothed, as is the calyx, with large, yellow, glandular scales. *Calyx* cut to the base into five very unequal linear lobes or segments, of which the upper one is much the longest, and almost subulate. *Corolla* small, infundibuliform, cinnabar-coloured, five-lobed, the *lobes* spreading, rounded, acute. *Ovary* oblong-ovate, glanduloso-squamose, five-celled. *Stamens* ten, included : *filaments* stout, hairy at the base. *Style* longer than the stamens, hairy below. *Stigma* capitate, five-lobed.

One of the most distinct of all the Indian Rhododendrons yet known, remarkable for its reticulated leaves and the singular colour and acute lobes of the corolla.

Tab. VIII. *Rhododendron cinnabarinum.* Fig. 1. Corolla. 2. Stamen. 3. Pistil and calyx. 4. Section of ovary, showing the five cells :—*magnified.*

9.

RHODODENDRON ELÆAGNOIDES, *Hook. fil.*

Oleaster-leaved Rhododendron.

Fruticulus ramosissimus, ramis tuberculatis subverticillatis, foliis parvis brevi-petiolatis late obovato-trapezoideis utrinque squamis orbiculatis dense furfuraceis, pedunculis solitariis fructiferis elongatis folia quintuplo superantibus, capsula oblongo-cylindracea 5-loculari 5-valvi basi segmentis calycinis $\frac{1}{4}$ brevioribus suffulta.

Hab. Mountains of Sikkim-Himalaya, at an elevation of 14–15,000 feet.

Frutex parvus lignosus valde ramosus ; ramis tortis divaricatis 4–8 uncias longis, cortice atro-fusco tuberculato tectis. *Folia* $\frac{1}{4}$ unciam longa, æquilata, coriacea, plana, obovato-trapezoidea, costa valida percursa, obtusa, basi in petiolum brevem angustata, utrinque squamulis minutis argenteo-furfuraceis ut in *Elæagno*. *Pedunculus* fructiferus uncialis, capsula erecta, 2 lineas longa.

A good many specimens of this plant were brought to me by my collectors from the neighbourhood of the snow in April, growing at about the elevation above stated ; but none in flower. A figure of it is therefore omitted ; and its affinities cannot of course be ascertained.

Tab. IX.

J.H.D. del. Fitch lith.

Reeve, Benham & Reeve, imp.

RHODODENDRON ARGENTEUM, Hook.fil.

10.

RHODODENDRON ARGENTEUM, *Hook. fil.*

Silvery Rhododendron.

TAB. IX.

Arboreum, foliis amplis subcoriaceis obovato-oblongis acutis in petiolum crassum attenuatis planis utrinque glaberrimis subtus argenteis costa nervisque prominulis, bracteis deciduis dense sericeis, pedunculis brevibus crassis puberulis, calyce brevissimo obscure lobato, corolla (inter maximas) alba late campanulata, limbi segmentis breviusculis bilobis, staminibus 10, filamentis glabris, ovarii pubescentis loculis subsedecim, stylo flexuoso crasso, stigmate dilatato.

HAB. Sikkim-Himalaya; summit of Sinchul, Suradah, and Tonglo, elev. 8,000–10,000 feet. *Fl.* April.

A *tree* thirty feet high: *trunks* solitary, or two or three together, spreading, branched above, the *bark* pale, the *branches* leafy at the apex. *Leaves* very beautiful in the leaf-buds, erect and silky, at first enveloped in large scales, so closely imbricated and so large, as to resemble the cones of some species of pine, the outer or lower scales broad and coriaceous, glabrous, coloured (reddish-brown), the innermost ones oblong-spathulate, pubescent. When fully developed the *leaves* are among the largest of the genus, six inches to a foot long, three to five inches broad, coriaceous, nearly plane, glabrous, full green above with parallel rather closely placed nerves, beneath silvery white, with the costa and nerves prominent. *Petioles* short. *Bracteas* deciduous, densely silky. *Flowers* two to three inches long, two to two and a half inches in diameter, always white.

In the silvery underside of the foliage, but in nothing else, this resembles *R. arboreum*; while in the much divided limb of the corolla, the ten-celled ovary, the stout flexuose style and large stigma, it approaches *R. Falconeri*, but only in those particulars. The blossoms are only second in size to *R. Dalhousiæ*. On Sinchul, the higher parts of the mountain, at from 8,000 to 9,000 feet of elevation, are more or less clothed with it: on Tonglo, as it approaches 10,000, it is suddenly replaced by the following species, *R. Falconeri*. It seems to be shy of flowering, this season at least (1848); for it was with difficulty I could procure sufficient specimens to complete my drawing.

TAB. IX. *Rhododendron argenteum*. Fig. 1. Stamen. 2. Pistil. 3. Section of ovary:—*magnified*.

Tab. X.

J. D. H. del. Fitch, lith.

Reeve Benham & Reeve imp.

RHODODENDRON FALCONERI, Hook. fil.

11.

RHODODENDRON FALCONERI, *Hook. fil.*

Dr. Falconer's Rhododendron.

TAB. X.

Arboreum, foliis amplis valde coriaceis obovato-ellipticis obtusis cum mucronulo basi cordatis supra nitidis glabris reticulatim venosis subtus ferrugineis costa petiolisque validis rufo-tomentoso-furfuraceis, capitulis globosis densis multifloris, pedunculis erectis pubescenti-viscosis, floribus parvis (pro planta) albis, calyce minutissimo vix lobato, corollæ lobis 10 rotundatis, staminibus 16, ovario hirsutissimo viscoso 18-loculari, stylo flexuoso incrassato longe exserto, stigmate dilatato.

HAB. Sikkim-Himalaya. Summit of Tonglo, elev. 10,000 feet.

A *tree* thirty feet in height; two or three *trunks* springing from the same point, and they are often two feet in diameter. The *bark* is pale and smooth: *branches* few, spreading, leafy at the points; the young leaves clothed with velvety down, and in the state of the bud concealed by downy glutinous scales, of which the outer are subulate, the inner ovate. The perfect *leaves* are very coriaceous, from eight inches to a foot in length, five to seven inches wide, the upper side glossy green, but fading into yellow at the margins, which margins are quite plane (not recurved), beneath, except on the mid-rib and reticulated veins, clothed with a short, dense, pale, ferruginous down. *Petioles* long and very thick, plane and glabrous above, semiterete and clothed with dark rusty down beneath. *Heads* not large, but composed of numerous, rather small, white, densely placed *flowers*. *Stamens* sixteen. *Style* much exserted. *Peduncles* erect, elongated after flowering. *Capsules* erect, eight to ten-valved, hispid, an inch and a half long, with numerous cells.

If not the most showy, this is certainly one of the most striking and distinct of the genus. The noble foliage has some resemblance to that of the variety of *Magnolia grandiflora*, which has the leaves ferruginous beneath. The dense many-flowered head, the multiplication of the lobes of the corolla, and of the stamens and cells of the fruit, and the exserted style, bring it very near *R. grande*, Wight's Ic. Plant., vol. iv. tab. 1202; but the foliage is totally different.

TAB. X. *Rhododendron Falconeri.* Fig. 1. Bracteal scale. 2. Flower. 3. Stamen. 4. Pistil. 5. Section of ovary:—*magnified*.

THE

RHODODENDRONS

OF

SIKKIM-HIMALAYA;

BEING

AN ACCOUNT, BOTANICAL AND GEOGRAPHICAL, OF THE

RHODODENDRONS RECENTLY DISCOVERED IN THE MOUNTAINS OF EASTERN HIMALAYA,

FROM

DRAWINGS AND DESCRIPTIONS MADE ON THE SPOT,

DURING A GOVERNMENT BOTANICAL MISSION TO THAT COUNTRY;

BY

JOSEPH DALTON HOOKER, R.N., M.D., F.R.S., F.L.S.,

&c., &c., &c.

EDITED BY

SIR W. J. HOOKER, K.H., D.C.L., F.R.S., F.L.S., &c.

Vice-President of the Linnean Society, and Director of the Royal Gardens of Kew.

PART II.

LONDON:

REEVE AND BENHAM, HENRIETTA STREET, COVENT GARDEN.

1851.

PREFACE.

IN the few remarks it seemed necessary to offer as introductory to the "Fasciculus of the Rhododendrons of Sikkim-Himalaya," we made the statement that the author of that work, during a limited sojourn in the country and under many difficulties and privations, had been able to detect there no less than eleven different species of *Rhododendron,* of which nine were considered new. A longer sojourn in the country, and more extended travels, and excursions to the more elevated regions of this vast mountain-chain, on the part of Dr. Hooker, have now brought to light no less than forty-three species, natives of Sikkim-Himalaya! many of which even exceed, in the size and beauty of their flowers or their foliage, the handsomest of those which had been previously discovered. Seeds, too, of a large proportion of these, have been sent to the Royal Gardens of Kew, and have arrived in so good a state, that we have been eminently successful in rearing them. Of all, accurate descriptions were drawn up on the spot; a great number of drawings were made, and Messrs. Reeve and Benham have readily acceded to the wish of the author to publish two more Fasciculi each of ten plates;—the plates executed with the same degree of skill and care, and coloured with the same fidelity to nature, as the preceding ones.

Not content with drawing and describing the species that fell under his own observation in India, Dr. Hooker has occupied himself with a hastily compiled *Conspectus* of all the species known to inhabit *continental India,* and in this we find forty-three species, arranged in eight groupes or divisions. This Conspectus we give in the present portion of the work, and by which it will be seen what species are to appear in the third and last Fasciculus.—ED.

ROYAL GARDENS, KEW,
February 1, 1851.

THE

RHODODENDRONS

OF

SIKKIM-HIMALAYA.

CONSPECTUS SPECIERUM INDIÆ ORIENTALIS.

I. *Calyx obsolete. Corolla broadly campanulate, hemispherical at the base. Stamens* 18–20 (*rarely* 10). *Ovary usually glanduloso-pubescent and villous, many* (10–20) *celled.—Trees. Leaves ample. Flowers white or pale purple, capitate, often crowded.*

1. R. *Falconeri,* Hook. fil. TAB. X.

HAB. Sikkim-Himalaya; outer and inner ranges. Mountain-tops and valleys. Elev. 10–12,000 feet.

Note. The natural size of the flowers of this species is often as great as that given for the magnified figure (fig. 2) in the plate quoted, in which case the capitula are fewer-flowered. Leaves often fifteen inches long and eight broad. Capsule densely villoso-tomentose, oblong-cylindrical, obtuse, slightly curved, an inch and a half long, half an inch wide. Seeds pale-brown.

2. R. *argenteum,* Hook. fil. TAB. IX.

HAB. Sikkim-Himalaya; inner and outer ranges. Elev. 8,000–10,000 feet. It flowered very abundantly in April of 1849.

Note. Stamens generally eighteen in number. Capsules puberulous, oblong-cylindrical, obtuse at both ends, one and a half to two inches long. Seeds pale.

3. R. *Hodgsoni,* Hook. fil. TAB. XV.

HAB. Sikkim-Himalaya. Elev. 10–12,000 feet.

4. R. *grande,* Wight, Icon. t. 1202.

HAB. Bhootan, *Griffith.*

B

II. *Calyx cupular, hemispherical or scutelliform, obsoletely lobed. Corolla campanulate, 5-lobed. Stamens 10–16. Ovary 6–16-celled.—Large flowering shrubs. Leaves very glabrous.*

5. R. *Aucklandii*, Hook. fil. TAB. XI.

HAB. Sikkim-Himalaya. Elev. 7–9,000 feet, rare.

6. R. *Griffithii*, Wight, Icon. t. 1203.

HAB. Bhootan, *Griffith*.

7. R. *Thomsoni*, Hook. fil. TAB. XII.

HAB. Sikkim-Himalaya. Elev. 11–13,000 feet, abundant.

8. R. *Candelabrum*, Hook. fil. TAB. XXIX.

HAB. Sikkim-Himalaya. Elev. 11–13,000 feet.

III. *Calyx subfoliaceous, 5-partite, lobes submembranaceous. Corolla infundibuliform or campanulate, tube elongated. Stamens 10–18. Ovary 5–6-celled.—Shrubs; frequently Epiphytes. Flowers white. Leaves generally lepidote beneath.*

9. R. *Dalhousiæ*, Hook. fil. TAB. I. II.

HAB. Sikkim-Himalaya; outer and inner ranges. Elev. 6,000–9,000 feet. *Fl.* May, June; *fr.* October.

Note. Gemmæ terminal, strobiliform, one and a half to two inches long; scales broad-orbicular, concave, very coriaceous, almost woody, pale-tawny, glabrous, ciliated towards the apex. Leaves glanduloso-punctate and rough with squamules. Petioles sometimes setose. Capsules large, woody, linear-oblong, rufous, slightly curved, muticous, 5-angled, punctato-glandulose, the valves linear, recurved at the apex, obscurely keeled at the back, the axis terminated by the persistent style. Seeds pale yellow.

10. R. *Edgeworthii*, Hook. fil. TAB. XXI.

HAB. Sikkim-Himalaya. Elev. 7–9,000 feet.

11. R. *barbatum*, Wall., Hook. fil. TAB. III.

HAB. Gossaing-Than, Nepal, *Wallich*. Sikkim-Himalaya. On spurs of mountains, and in valleys. Elev. 9,000–11,000 feet.

Note. Branches, peduncles, and calyces glabrous or setose. Leaves beneath quite glabrous or sub-villous. Capsules generally glandulose, rarely quite glabrous, glands stipitate. Very variable in the degree of hairiness, but otherwise a well-marked species.

12. R. *lancifolium*, Hook. fil. TAB. IV.

HAB. Sikkim-Himalaya. Elev. 8–10,000 feet.

Note. Probably only a glabrous small-flowered and small-leaved variety of *R. barbatum*.

13. R. *ciliatum*, Hook. fil. (n. sp.) TAB. XXIV.

HAB. Sikkim-Himalaya. Lachen and Lachoong valleys. Elev. 9–10,000 feet.

14. R. *glaucum*, Hook. fil. TAB. XVII.

HAB. Sikkim-Himalaya. Chola, Lachen, and Lachoong passes. Elev. 10–12,000 feet.

15. R. *vaccinioides*, Hook. fil. (n. sp.); fruticulus laxe vage ramosus, caulibus ramisque gracilibus tuberculatis ultimis petiolis pedunculis foliisque subtus sparse squamulosis, foliis coriaceis obovatis obtusis emarginatisve superne glaberrimis subter pallidioribus, pedicellis subterminalibus solitariis gracilibus, lobis calycinis ovatis obtusis, capsula parva gracili curvata 5-loculari, valvis submembranaceis.

HAB. Sikkim-Himalaya; epiphytal, or growing on moist rocks, in very damp places, on the inner and outer ranges. Alt. 6–8,000 feet. *Fl.* ?

A small, very slender, straggling species, sometimes pendulous from trunks of trees, and then two feet long, of of a bright green colour, and so like a common Sikkim species of *Vaccinium* (*V. obovatum*, Wight, Icon. t. 1193) as not to be distinguishable at first sight.

Stems no thicker than a dove's quill, scabrid with tubercles, indicating the former position of scales, which still clothe the ramuli, petioles, and, more sparingly, the under surface of the foliage. *Leaves* coriaceous, three-fourths to one inch long, obovate or even spathulate, the lamina produced downwards to the very base of the petiole; upper surface a bright green, lower paler. *Peduncles* of the fruit as long as the leaves, slender. *Calyx* small, but manifestly foliaceous. *Capsules* curving, narrow, pale-coloured, and membranous, an inch long, scarce one-eighth of an inch in diameter, valves linear, torulose, a little scaly on the back. *Seeds* pale-coloured.

I have never found the flowers of this singular and very distinct little species.

16. R. *pumilum*, Hook. fil. TAB. XIV.

HAB. Sikkim-Himalaya. Zemu and T'hlonok rivers, rare. Elev. 12–14,000 feet.

IV. *Calyx small or obsolete, rarely 5-toothed, lobes equal. Corolla campanulate, or with the limb contracted below its base, and subinfundibuliform. Stamens* 10. *Ovary* 5–10-*celled.—Shrubs, generally glabrous or clothed beneath, sometimes lepidote.*

17. R. *arboreum*, Sm. *Exot. Flora*, t. 6. (supra p. 6), *not Wight, Ic.* t. 1201.

HAB. Himalaya Mountains: from Bhootan to the western extremity. Elev. 5–8,000 feet.

18. R. *Campbelliæ*, Hook. fil. TAB. VI. R. Nilagiricum, *Hook. Bot. Mag.* t. 4381 (*not Zenker*).—*var.* β. flore albo. R. arboreum, album, *Wall. Ic. Rar. Ind. Or.* vol. ii. p. 23. t. 123 ?

HAB. Sikkim-Himalaya; on both the outer and inner ranges, at elevations of from 7–10,—and even 11,000 feet.—β. Mountain of Sheopore in Nepal. *Dr. Wallich.*

Note. It has been already stated that the chief difference between this and *R. arboreum* consisted in the rusty dull (unpolished) tomentum of the underside of the leaf of *R. Campbelliæ*, as compared with the silvery compact filmy clothing of the latter. Dr. T. Thomson assures me that in Western Himalaya, where *R. arboreum* is so common, it is never otherwise than silvery and white beneath. Since I have seen the figure of *R. Nilagiricum* in the Botanical Magazine, Tab. 4381, I am quite disposed to consider the present species identical with that, exactly agreeing with that in the shape of the leaves, as well as in other characters, and since that is acknowledged to have differently-formed leaves from the true *R. Nilagiricum* of Zenker, and also said to be from Nepal, not from the Neelgherries, we can hardly doubt but that it may safely be brought as a synonym to our *R. Campbelliæ*: perhaps, also, Dr. Wallich's *R. nobile* (Wall. Cat. n. 1521, excluding 2) is not different, but this is nowhere accurately described, and possibly *R. cinnamomeum* (which by many is considered a variety of *R. arboreum*) of the same author, from Nepal. I have not seen *R. Campbelliæ* below 7,000 feet, whereas *R. arboreum, verum*, ranges from 5,000 to 8,000 feet.

19. R. *Nilagiricum*, Zenker, *Plant. Nilag. cum Ic.* (*not Hook. Bot. Mag.* t. 4381). R. arboreum, *Wight, Ic.* t. 1201 (*not Sm.*) R. nobile, *Wall. Cat.* n. 1521. 2 (*not* 1).

HAB. Neelgherry hills, abundant. *Wight, Zenker, and others.*

Note. Difficult as it may be to define the characters of this species in words, yet we believe that no one can see our native specimens in the herbarium without feeling assured that it is a distinct species, and truly different from any found in the north of India. There is a peculiarity in the firm and hard texture of the broad foliage, with its strongly recurved margins, and the deeply impressed venation and opake green colour; and a still stronger distinguishing mark is in the almost globose strobilus, formed by the scales of the united flowers while in young bud, and which is admirably represented in Dr. Wight's plate above quoted. The nearest approach to this is in the *Rhododendron* from Adam's Peak and other mountains of Ceylon, which, I believe, has never been described, though it has been considered, while there was believed to be only one *tree* Rhododendron in India, as *R. arboreum*, and it is cultivated in nurseries under the name of *R. Zeylanicum*. This has darker foliage than *R. Nilagiricum*, and is much larger in all its parts.

20. R. *nobile*, Wall. *Cat.* n. 1521 (not 2, which is *R. Nilagiricum*).

HAB. Kamaon. *Dr. Wallich.*

21. R. *niveum*, Hook. fil.; arbuscula vage ramosa, cortice fusco rugoso, ramulis pubescentibus, foliis obovato-lanceolatis breve petiolatis obtusis v. subacutis super glaberrimis opacis subter petioloque tomento appresso niveo (rarius fuscescente) lanatis, capitulis densissimis, pedicellis brevibus, calyce obsoleto, capsulis oblongo-cylindraceis tomentosis utrinque obtusis 6-locularibus, valvis lignosis, seminibus pallidis.

HAB. Sikkim-Himalaya; rocky valleys and ridges, Lachen, Lachoong, and Chola; elev. 10–12,000 feet, not unfrequent. *Fl.* ? *Fr.* November.

A small rugged-barked tree, having the habit and general appearance of *R. arboreum*, with which and *R. Campbelliæ* it grows frequently intermixed, but may be distinguished, even at a distance, by the snow-white under-surface of the leaf. On a closer inspection this is seen to be caused by an appressed flocculent tomentum, occupying both surfaces of the very young leaf, and sometimes of a rusty-red hue. In the two quoted allies the the leaf is narrower and the whitish hue or silvery lustre of the under-surface of the leaf is not removable, and is generally shining. The upper surface of the leaf of this is opake, but in *R. Campbelliæ*, polished. *Capsules* of this shorter, more cylindrical, blunt, and straight. I have never known these species to pass into one another. The present inhabits a much higher elevation than that usually occupied by *R. arboreum*. The flowers I have never seen.

22. R. *formosum*, Wall., *Pl. Asiat. Rar.* vol. iii. p. 207. *Hook. Bot. Mag.* t. 4457. R. Gibsoni, *Hortulan.*

HAB. Mountains bordering on Silhet. *Dr. Wallich, Mr. Griffith*, and *Mr. Gibson.*

23. R. *campanulatum*, Don, *Wern. Trans.* vol. iii. p. 409. *Wall. Cat.* n. 756. *Hook. Bot. Mag.* t. 1944.

HAB. Gossaing-Than in Nepal; and Kamaon. *Wallich, Hamilton.*

24. R. *Wallichii*, Hook. fil. TAB. V.

HAB. Sikkim-Himalaya; on spurs and in valleys of the inner and outer ranges; elev. 11–13,000 feet. *Fl.* June; *fr.* October.

Note. Distinguished from *R. campanulatum* by the conspicuous calyx. Leaves ferruginous or olivaceous beneath, pubescent or villous. Capsules linear, slightly curved, nearly erect, woody, glabrous, an inch to an inch and a half long. Seeds pale.

25. R. *Wightii*, Hook. fil. TAB. XXVII.

HAB. Sikkim-Himalaya. Elev. 12–14,000 feet.

26. R. *lanatum*, Hook. fil. TAB. XVI.

HAB. Sikkim-Himalaya, at Jongri and Chola. Elev. 10–12,000 feet.

27. R. *fulgens*, Hook. fil. TAB. XXV.

HAB. Sikkim-Himalaya. Elev. 12–14,000 feet.

28. R. *æruginosum*, Hook. fil. TAB. XXII.

HAB. Sikkim-Himalaya. Elev. 12–14,000 feet.

29. R. *campylocarpum*, Hook. fil. TAB. XXX.

HAB. Sikkim-Himalaya. Elev. 11–14,000 feet.

V. *Calyx short, coriaceous, 5-lobed or 5-dentate, lobes short, one (the upper) generally elongated, sometimes subulate. Corolla funnel-shaped, tube narrowed, lobes rounded or acute. Stamens* 10–20. *Ovary* 5–10-*celled.—Shrubs. Leaves lepidote beneath. Flowers closely capitate.*

30. R. *Maddeni*, Hook. fil. TAB. XVIII.

HAB. Sikkim-Himalaya. Lachen and Lachoong valleys, very rare. Elev. 6,000 feet.

31. R. *cinnabarinum*, Hook. fil. TAB. VIII.

HAB. Sikkim-Himalaya; chiefly in valleys and on the skirts of woods, elev. 10–12,000 feet, abundant. *Fl.* June; *fr.* November.

Note. Shrub six feet high, very elegant; branches and branchlets virgate. Corymb spreading. Peduncles half an inch long. Flowers pendent. Capsules small, half an inch long, ovate, obtuse.—One of the most elegant species of the genus, but very inefficiently represented at our Tab. VIII. Its pendulous or drooping flowers, when in perfection, are peculiarly graceful. It is universally considered poisonous to cattle and goats: of the latter I have seen many die, from eating either of this or of a species of *Andromeda*;—which latter is notorious for this property throughout Sikkim, Nepal, and N. W. Himalaya. If employed for fuel, the smoke of *R. cinnabarinum* causes the eyes to inflame and the cheeks to swell.

32. R. *Roylei*, Hook. fil. TAB. VII.

HAB. Sikkim-Himalaya. Elev. 10–11,000 feet.

Note. Very near, it must be confessed, to *R. cinnabarinum*.

VI. *Calyx subfoliaceous,* 5-*partite, lobes coriaceous or membranaceous. Tube of the corolla short, tinged at the base, the lobes patent, concave. Stamens* 8–10. *Style subclavate, short, decurved, valid. Stigma thickened, disciform. Ovary* 5-*celled.—Shrubs, often small, epiphytes or terrestrial. Leaves (except in* R. pendulum) *densely lepidote.*

33. R. *camelliæflorum*, Hook. fil. TAB. XXVIII.

HAB. Sikkim-Himalaya; generally pendent from the trunks of trees, sometimes rocks. Elev. 9–11,000 feet.

C

34. R. *pendulum*, Hook. fil. TAB. XIII.

HAB. Sikkim-Himalaya; pendulous from trees, generally, rarely from rocks. Elev. 9–11,000 feet.

35. R. *obovatum*, Hook. fil.; frutex ramosus, ramis ramulisque gracilibus, ramulis pedunculis calyce corolla extus petiolis foliisque subtus (junioribus utrinque) sparse squamuloso-ferrugineis, foliis petiolatis obovatis basi in petiolum angustatis apice rotundatis apiculatis vix coriaceis marginibus planis superne opacis subtus pallide ochraceo-brunneis, pedunculis brevibus (fructiferis elongatis) terminalibus solitariis, calycis lobis foliaceis obtusis, corolla rubro-purpurea (ut in *R. lepidoto*), staminibus 8, filamentis basi sericeo-villosis, ovario creberrime lepidoto, stylo brevi crasso, capsulis conico-ovatis abrupte truncatis 5-sulcatis 5-locularibus, valvis lignosis lepidotis.

HAB. Sikkim-Himalaya; rocky places. Lachoong valley, 12,000 feet. *Fl.* June, and again partially in September; *fr.* November.

A small shrub, 3–4 feet high, much branched, and very resinous in odour. *Branches* as stout as a duck's quill, not tortuous, but much divided, the upper scabrid where once lepidote. *Leaves* plane, membranous for the genus, of an opake green above and pale yellow-brown below, the *costa* slender, percurrent; lamina an inch and a half long, half to three-quarters of an inch broad. *Buds* nearly globular; scales orbicular, coriaceous, brown, downy on the outer surface, ciliated, the outer ones lepidote. *Pedicels* half to three-quarters of an inch long, one to one and a half inch when in fruit, very lepidote, as is the calyx, base of the corolla, and ovarium, and fruit. *Corolla* altogether like that of *R. lepidotum*. *Capsules* one-fourth to one-third of an inch long, about twice the length of the persistent calyx-lobes.

The form and size of the foliage, and its glabrous upper surface, distinguish this well from *R. lepidotum*.

[There is no original drawing of this species.—*Ed.*]

36. R. *salignum*, Hook. fil. TAB. XXIII. A.

HAB. Sikkim-Himalaya; above Choongtam. Elev. 7,000 feet.

37. R. *elæagnoides*, Hook. fil. (supra Fasc. I. p. 8. n. 9). TAB. XXIII. B.

HAB. Sikkim-Himalaya; open rocky places. Elev. 12–16,000 feet.

38. R. *lepidotum*, Wall., *Cat.* n. 738. *Royle, Ill.* p. 260. t. 64. f. 1.

HAB. High mountains, Nepal, *Dr. Wallich*, *Dr. Royle*. Sikkim-Himalaya, elev. 12–15,000 feet, *J. D. H.*

Note. A small densely-tufted shrub, a foot or so high, allied to *R. elæagnoides* and *R. obovatum*, with the flowers always on very short petioles. Its common name is "*Tsaluma*," or "*Tsuma*," amongst the Bhoteas, and its resinous odour is very strong, not unpleasant. The description in De Candolle (Prodr. v. 7. p. 724), if, as I do not doubt, it refers to this plant, is very erroneous. The leaves cannot be called "ferruginous below," in the same sense as applied to *R. anthopogon*, &c.; nor are there any setæ or cilia at the bases of the leaves; nor have I observed more than eight stamens, the typical number in this very distinct group, which includes *R. salignum*, *R. obovatum*, and *R. elæagnoides*. The flowers vary from very fine red to a dingy yellow.

VII. *Calyx subfoliaceous, 5-partite or 5-lobed, lobes short, rounded. Tube of the corolla short, funnel-shaped, lobes of the limb elongated, narrow, spreading, entire. Stamens* 8, *exserted: filaments elongated, slender. Style slender, much exserted. Ovary* 5-*celled.—Lepidote shrubs.*

39. R. *triflorum*, Hook. fil. TAB. XIX.

HAB. Sikkim-Himalaya. Elev. 7–9,000 feet; scarce.

40. R. *virgatum*, Hook. fil. TAB. XXVI. A.

HAB. Sikkim-Himalaya; skirts of Pine-forests. Elev. 8–9,000 feet.

41. R. *nivale*, Hook. fil. TAB. XXVI. B.

HAB. Sikkim-Himalaya; on the loftiest bare slopes on the Thibetan frontier. Elev. 16–18,000 feet.

42. R. *setosum*, Hook. fil. TAB. XX.

HAB. Sikkim-Himalaya; open stony and rocky places. Elev. 13–16,000 feet.

VIII. *Calyx* 5-*phyllous, lobes membranaceous. Corolla hypocrateriform, tube narrow, cylindrical, limb plane, patent. Stamens* 6–8, *included. Style short, clavate. Ovary* 5-*celled.—Small lepidote shrubs.*

43. R. *anthopogon*, Don, *Trans. Wern. Soc.* vol. iii. p. 409. *Hook. Bot. Mag.* t. 3947. R. aromaticum, *Wall. Cat.* n. 1520.

HAB. Gossaing-Than, Nepal, and Kamaon, *Wallich, Hamilton*; Sikkim-Himalaya: rocky, open, especially gravelly places, abundant. Elev. 12–16,000 feet.

Note. A strongly and far more disagreeably and heavily odorous plant than *R. setosum.* This, the *Palu* of the Bhoteas, shares with the *Tsallu* (*R. setosum*) the blame of exciting the headache and nausea attending ascents to the dreaded elevations of the Eastern Himalaya. In the Herbarium its permanent odour is more disagreeable than that of any of the genus. Nothing, however, can exceed the beauty of its flowers, whether we consider the exquisitely tender, membranaceous, translucent texture of the corolla, with its delicate nervation, or the rich blush of the first opening blossoms, which insensibly passes into snowy white, then faintly tinged with sulphur—all colours seen on one and the same plant.

Tab. XI

J.D.H. del. Fitch, lith.

RHODODENDRON AUCKLANDII, Hook. fil.

Reeve, Benham & Reeve, imp.

12.

RHODODENDRON AUCKLANDII, *Hook. fil.*

Lord Auckland's Rhododendron.

TAB. XI.

Frutex, cortice lævi pallido subpapyraceo, foliis amplis sublonge petiolatis oblongo-ovalibus acutis basi cordatis margine planis subtus vix glaucescentibus coriaceis venis divaricatis, floribus (inter maximos) 3–5 terminalibus albis, pedunculis longiusculis, calyce patelliformi-subrhomboideo inæqualiter obscure lobato, corollæ tubo late campanulato, limbo amplissimo patente, lobis 5 rotundatis emarginato-bifidis, staminibus 12–18, ovario glanduloso 12-loculari, stylo valido curvato, stigmate magno disciformi, capsula oblongo-cylindracea coriacea utrinque obtusa, valvis crassis dorso glaberrimis.

HAB. Sikkim-Himalaya; inner ranges only; elevation 7–9,000 feet, rare. *Fl.* May and June. *Fr.* October.

Seen in scattered *bushes*, four to eight feet high, branching from the base: and there the trunk is six inches in diameter. *Branches* suberect, copiously leafy. *Bark* smooth and papery. *Wood* resembling that of *R. Hodgsoni*. *Leaves* variable in size and breadth, but large for the size of the plant, four to ten inches long, coriaceous, oblong-elliptical, scarcely approaching to lanceolate, acute, cordate at the base, penninerved, the *nerves* patent, the margin plane often tinged with yellow, upper surface light full green, the under paler, slightly glaucescent, everywhere glabrous. *Petioles* two inches long. *Flowers* the largest of the genus, but variable in size, terminal, three to five together, inodorous. *Peduncles* rather slender, longer than the petioles, red or green. The *calyx* represents a shallow, concave, irregular, subrhomboid-shaped platter, an inch and a half in its longest diameter, obscurely lobed, upper lobe most elongated, the back marked with slightly elevated, radiating lines, glossy, as it were varnished. *Corolla* pure white, tinged with pink, veiny, of a firm, rather fleshy, texture: *tube* short for the size of the flower, yellowish and rose-colour towards the base, the mouth very wide, limb exceedingly large and spreading: we have measured some only three inches across, but others five inches and five inches and a half in diameter! *Stamens* twelve to eighteen, small for so large a flower: *filaments* glabrous; *anthers* obovate, ochreous brown. *Ovary* ovate, rather short, glaucous green, granulated. *Style* rather flexuose, curving upwards, terminating in a spreading, concave disc, from which the hemispherical lobed *stigma* rises. *Capsule* an inch and a half long, three-quarters of an inch broad.

It has been my lot to discover but few plants of this superb species, and in these the inflorescence varied much in size. The specimens from which our drawing was made were from a bush which grew in a rather dry sunny exposure, above the village of Choongtam, and the bush was covered with blossoms. The same species also grows on the skirts of the Pine-forests (*Abies Brunoniana*) above Lamteng, and it is there conspicuous for the abundance rather than for the large size of its blossoms.

To this fine plant I have the melancholy satisfaction of affixing the name of the late Right Honourable Lord Auckland, no less in token of my gratitude for the kindness and patronage I received from him, when First Lord of the Admiralty, than in memory of his zealous promotion of every scientific inquiry, and his liberal patronage of the arts and sciences while he filled the exalted station of Governor-General of India.

TAB. XI. *Rhododendron Aucklandii.* Fig. 1. Stamen. 2. Pistil. 3. Section of ovary:—*slightly magnified.* 4. Fruit:—*natural size.*

Tab. XII.

J.D.H. del. Fitch lith.

Reeve Benham & Reeve, imp.

RHODODENDRON THOMSONI, Hook fil.

13.

RHODODENDRON THOMSONI, *Hook. fil.*

Dr. Thomson's Rhododendron.

TAB. XII.

Frutex ramosissimus, cortice pallide papyraceo, foliis in ramos terminales coriaceis glaberrimis orbiculari-ovatis obtusissimis apiculatis basi cordatis læte virentibus subtus glaucescentibus margine subrecurvo, petiolo gracili, corymbis plurifloris, pedunculis longitudine petiolorum, floribus radiatim patentibus cernuisve, calyce amplo cylindraceo-cyathiformi basi retuso inæqualiter lobato, lobis erectis obtusissimis, corolla intense sanguinea coriaceo-carnosa nitida, tubo elongato-campanuliformi, limbi lobis 5 patenti-subrecurvis profunde emarginatis superioribus intus maculatis, staminibus 10, ovario conico-cylindraceo glaberrimo 6–10-loculari, stylo gracili, stigmate conico, capsula calyce cylindraceo persistente $\frac{3}{4}$ tecta.

HAB. Sikkim-Himalaya; inner and outer ranges; elev. 11–13,000 feet; abundant. *Fl.* June. *Fr.* November.

A *bush* six to ten feet high, or in damp woods fifteen feet, but then spare, and woody. Lower *branches* stout, a foot in diameter; upper slender, leafy at the extremities. *Leaves* two to three inches long, very broad, generally orbicular-ovate, but sometimes almost exactly orbicular, much resembling those of *R. campylocarpum*, Hook. fil., only that in the latter the petioles are often glandular, here never; the texture of the leaves is coriaceous, but not very thick, the apex very blunt, tipped with a short mucro, the base subcordate, the colour pale green, below subglaucous, everywhere quite glabrous. *Flowers* in a corymb of six to eight together from the apices of short branches among the leaves, on peduncles an inch or more long, which radiate, as it were, from a centre, spreading horizontally or curving downwards. *Calyx* large, between cylindrical and hemispherical, or deep cup-shaped, coloured red in the upper half, green below, the base intruse for the reception of the peduncle, three-quarters of an inch long and as much wide, the mouth almost truncate but obscurely lobed. *Corolla* remarkable for the almost unrivalled deep blood-red colour and glossy surface of its flowers, yielding only to *R. fulgens*, Hook. fil.,—deeper coloured than that of *R. arboreum*: the *tube* elongated, often vertically compressed, two inches long; the *limb* large, much spreading, five-lobed, the *lobes* emarginate, upper ones spotted. *Stamens* a little longer than the tube: *filaments* glabrous, white; *anthers* rather large, deep brown. *Ovary* conico-cylindrical, glabrous, furrowed, six- to eight-celled. *Capsule* rather short, straight, glaucous purple, about three-quarters of its length immersed in the persistent calyx.

The whole is perfectly inodorous. Much honey is secreted in the base of the corolla, which has the character of not being poisonous, like what is yielded by *R. Dalhousiæ* and *R. argenteum*. The two latter species are said to render wild honey, collected in spring (their flowering season), deleterious.

To this species I give the name of Dr. Thomas Thomson, surgeon, H. E. I. C. S., late of the Thibetian Mission, son of the learned Professor of Chemistry of Glasgow University, my earliest friend and companion during my College life, and now my valued travelling companion in Eastern Himalaya.

TAB. XII. *Rhododendron Thomsoni.* Fig. 1. Stamen. 2. Pistil. 3. Transverse section of ovary:—*magnified.*

Tab. XIII.

J.D.H. del. Fitch lith.

Reeve Benham & Reeve imp.

RHODODENDRON PENDULUM, Hook. fil.

14.

RHODODENDRON PENDULUM, *Hook. fil.*

Pendulous Rhododendron.

TAB. XIII.

Fruticulus epiphytus pendulus, caulibus gracillimis dichotome ramosis, ramulis pedunculis petiolis brevibus foliisque subter (junioribus utrinque) tomento fulvo laxo dense vestitis, foliis elliptico-oblongis subacutis apiculatis convexis superne nitidis, pedunculis terminalibus subbinis rarius axillaribus parvis, calyce profunde 5-lobo hirsuto, lobis ellipticis submembranaceis æqualibus, corollæ albæ extus lepidotæ tubo brevissimo, limbo patente 5-lobo, lobis æqualibus subundulatis integris, staminibus 10, filamentis (nunc 2–3 basi inter se coalitis) rectis inferne dilatatis supra medium dense barbatis, antheris magnis obovatis, ovario parvo densissime fulvo-villoso, capsula brevi calycem persistentem vix superante villosa basi lepidota.

HAB. Sikkim-Himalaya; pendulous from the limbs of tall Pine-trees (*Abies Webbiana* and *Brunoniana*); elev. 9–11,000 feet, rarely found upon rocks; often covered with *Usnea*.

Stems three to four feet long, sparingly but dichotomously branched, *branches* scarcely stouter than a crow's quill: young shoots very villous. *Leaves* chiefly confined to the apices of the ultimate branches, on short *petioles*, spreading, between elliptical and oblong, acute or nearly so, and further tipped with a short mucro, smooth (never lepidote) and shining above, the margins a little recurved, an inch and a half to two inches long, and about three-quarters of an inch broad, below densely clothed with ferruginous tomentum. *Scales* of the flower-buds coriaceous, the outer lepidote, the inner villous. *Peduncles* two or three from the apex of the young leafy branches, very short, but longer than the petioles, ferruginously villous, bearing one or two linear *bracteas*. *Flowers* small. *Calyx* large in proportion to the size of the flower, deeply cut into five, oval, membranaceous lobes, lepidote below, villous. *Corolla* pure white, about an inch in diameter, externally lepidote, tube very short, gradually expanding into the nearly equally five-lobed *limb*: *lobes* rotundate, waved at the margin, entire. *Stamens* ten: *filaments* straight, sometimes more or less combined at the base, and there dilated; below the middle is a dense mass of white hairs; *anthers* large in proportion to the flower. *Ovary* ovate, densely villous, lepidote towards the base. *Style* very short, curved upwards, and thickened beneath the *stigma*, which is a convex, scarcely lobed *disc*. *Capsule* broadly ovate, acute, hairy, four to five lines long, five-celled, five-valved.

This species is inodorous, very distinct, but clearly allied to *R. camelliæflorum*, Hook. fil., the lepidote character of that species giving place to a denser fulvous or ferruginous tomentum here. In the size and colour and regular lobes of the corolla, and also in the general form of the calyx, the present may be compared with the *R. albiflorum** of the Rocky Mountains of North America, but in little else. Growing, as it does, an epiphyte, upon the trunks of trees in the gloomy and almost impenetrable forests, it is a plant very difficult of detection.

* Hook. Fl. Bor. Am. vol. ii. p. 43. f. 133.

TAB. XIII. *Rhododendron pendulum.* Fig. 1. Flower. 2. Stamens. 3. Pistil. 4. Transverse section of ovary:—*magnified.* 5. Capsule with its persistent calyx:—*natural size.*

Tab XIV.

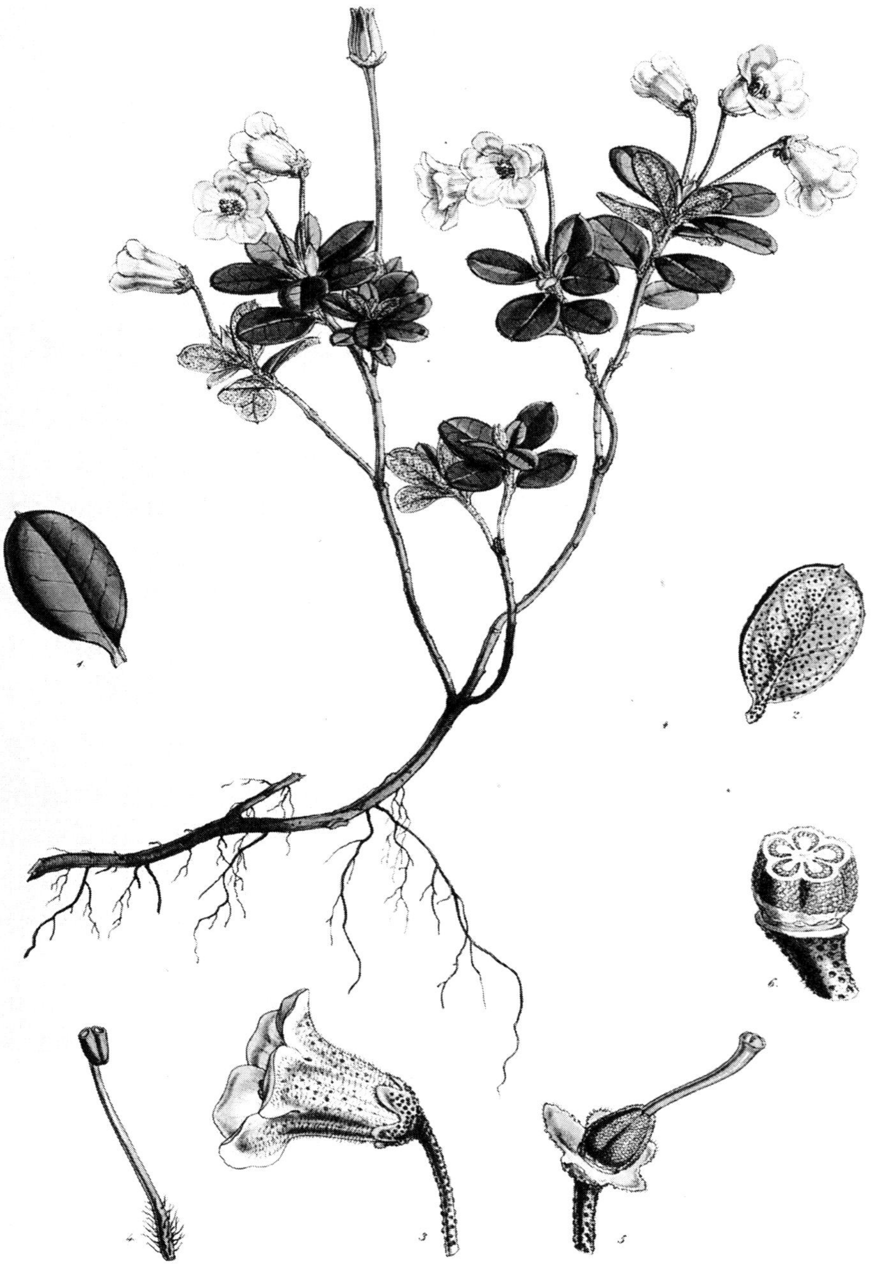

J.D.H. del. Fitch lith.

Frederic Reeve imp.

RHODODENDRON PUMILUM, Hook. fil.

15.

RHODODENDRON PUMILUM, *Hook. fil.*

Dwarf Rhododendron.

TAB. XIV.

Fruticulus humilis laxe ramosus, ramulis foliis subter petiolis pedunculis calycibus ovariisque lepidotis, foliis parvis brevi-petiolatis lato-ellipticis coriaceis apiculatis superne glaberrimis subter precipue glaucis, pedunculis solitariis 2–3-nis elongatis erectis strictis, flore inclinato, calycis lobis ovatis obtusis, corollæ roseæ campanulatæ extus pubescentis tubo elongato, limbi lobis brevibus rotundatis integris, staminibus 10 inclusis, filamentis rectis basi hispidis, stylo rectiusculo, stigmate capitato, capsula in pedunculum magis elongatum erecta ovata 5-loculari calycem persistentem multoties superante.

HAB. Sikkim-Himalaya; on alpine slopes among ericaceous vegetation, rare; about the Zemu and Thlonok rivers. *Fl.* June.

The smallest of all the Sikkim Rhododendrons: its slender woody *stem* roots among moss, *Andromeda fastigiata*, &c., ascends obliquely, and bears a few somewhat spreading dichotomous branches, three to four inches in length, rising above the surrounding vegetation. *Leaves* chiefly from the upper ends of the branches, half to three-quarters of an inch long, broadly elliptical, rigid, mucronate, smooth and naked and bright bluish-green above, below lepidote, as is the short petiole, and glaucous. *Bracts* of the flower-buds coriaceous, smooth and downy, and, as is usual in the lepidote species, quite destitute of glands or squamulæ. *Peduncles* moderately slender, erect, one to three from the apex of the branches, and rising an inch and a half above the base of the superior leaves, firm and woody, much elongated, and strict to the very apex in fruit. *Flower* inclined or almost drooping. *Calyx-lobes* rather short, but somewhat leafy in texture, reddish-brown, scaly, particularly towards the base. *Corolla* half to three-quarters of an inch long, rose-colour, campanulate, very delicate, externally all over down, and obscurely glandular: the *tube* rather broad, the *limb* of five, nearly equal, moderately spreading roundish *lobes*, which are quite entire. *Stamens* ten, included: *filaments* nearly straight, hispid at the base. *Ovary* ovate, densely lepidote, five-celled. *Style* rather short, thickened upwards. *Stigma* capitate, obscurely five-lobed. *Capsule* perfectly erect on the elongated strict peduncle, three-quarters of an inch long, large for the size of the plant, ovate, red-brown, five-valved.

Although the smallest among the Sikkim-Himalayan Rhododendrons, it is an extremely elegant species, and apparently of very rare occurrence: for I have never gathered it but twice, and each time in the wild district above indicated, where its elegant flowers are produced soon after the snow has melted: and then its pretty pink bells are seen peeping above the surrounding short heath-like vegetation, reminding the botanist of those of *Linnæa borealis.*

It yields a faint and agreeable odour, like that of *R. glaucum,* to which this has many points of resemblance.

TAB. XIV. *Rhododendron pumilum.* Fig. 1. Upper side of a leaf. 2. Under side. 3. Flower. 4. Stamen. 5. Calyx and pistil. 6. Transverse section of ovary:—*magnified.*

Tab. XV.

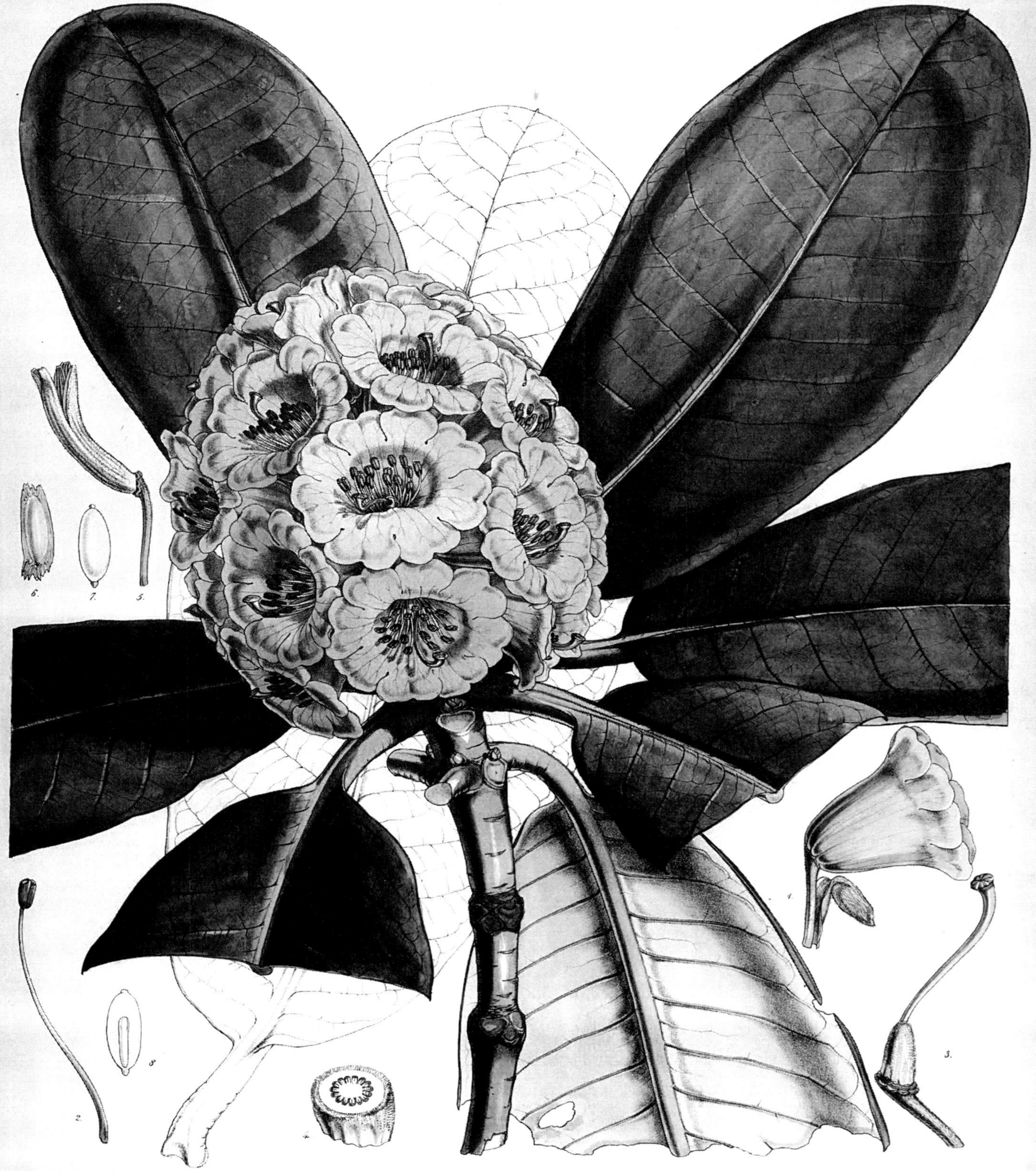

J. D. H. del. Fitch lith.

RHODODENDRON HODGSONI, Hook. fil.

16.

RHODODENDRON HODGSONI, *Hook. fil.*

Mr. Hodgson's Rhododendron.

TAB. XV.

Arborescens, ramis lævibus, foliis amplis petiolatis (petiolis crassis) obovato-ellipticis obtusis basi subcordatis coriaceis glaberrimis marginibus recurvis læte viridibus subtus tomento appresso subargenteo albido-glaucescentibus, capitulis magnis 15–30-floris, pedunculis brevibus tomentosis, calyce obsoleto, corollæ roseæ tubo (basi intruso) late campanulato, limbo brevi 8-lobo, lobis rotundatis æqualibus emarginatis, staminibus sub-18, filamentis gracilibus glabris, ovario pube viscido dense vestito 16-loculari, stylo elongato, stigmate disciformi radiatim lobato, capsulis anguste cylindraceis elongatis curvatis obtusis tomentosis.

HAB. Sikkim-Himalaya; on rocky spurs, and in the valleys of the outer and inner ranges; elev. 10–12,000 feet, very abundant. *Fl.* May and June; *fr.* December.

A small *tree*, from twelve feet, the average height, to twenty, branching from the base, main branches as thick as the human thigh, spreading horizontally for twenty or thirty feet each way, interwoven with the adjacent plants and shrubs. *Bark* smooth, papery, pale-flesh coloured, flaking off in broad membranous patches. *Wood* white, very close-grained, soft, yet tough, neither warping nor splitting, but, in consequence of the great compression of the larger branches, rarely affording a sample a foot in the square. *Leaf-buds* or *gemmæ* terminal, as large as a hazel-nut; their scales broadly ovate, concave, coriaceous, subtomentose, tapering into a long acuminated point. *Leaves* terminal on the ultimate branches, ample, spreading, twelve to sixteen and often eighteen inches in length, varying in form, oblong-elliptical or obovate or ovate-lanceolate, obtuse, nearly cordate at the base, of a singularly thick coriaceous texture, quite glabrous and bright glossy green above, penninerved (scarcely reticulated), the margins recurved; beneath, all, except the thickened costa, clothed with a pale silvery white, rarely ferruginous, closely appressed *tomentum*, but which is easily abraded by the finger, and is often itself evanescent. *Petioles* one to two inches or more long, very stout. *Capitula* four to six inches in diameter, of several delicate, pale purple or rose-coloured *flowers*. *Peduncles* short, viscid, often downy. *Calyx* obsolete. *Corolla* large, the tube an inch and a half long, broadly campanulate, the base depressed at the insertion upon the peduncle, the margin of the depression lobed, limb spreading, two to two and a half inches across, eight-lobed, the lobes rather short, emarginate, or obtusely bifid, reflexed. *Stamens* sixteen to eighteen, spreading: *filaments* slender, glabrous; *anthers* rather small, dark purple-brown. *Ovary* oblong-ovate, densely covered with a short, white, viscid *tomentum*, many-celled. *Style* rather short, glabrous, thickened upwards. *Stigma* a broad radiately-lobed disc. *Capsules* slightly curved, two inches long, cylindrical, striated, covered with a white loose tomentum. *Seeds* small, winged with a lax aril, jagged at both ends.

This, and the *Abies Webbiana*, I have always regarded as the characteristic tree and shrub (or underwood) at the elevation of 10 to 12,000 feet in all the valleys of Sikkim. *R. Hodgsoni*, in this respect, ranks with the *R. arboreum* and *Campbelliæ*, being typical of a loftier zone of Rhododendrons, succeeded by the arctic one of *R. anthopogon*, *R. setosum*, *R. elæagnoides*, and, finally, far above the ordinary limit of phænogamic vegetation, by *R. nivale*, which is found at an elevation of 18,000 feet above the level of the sea.

Nowhere can the traveller wander, in the limits assigned to the present species, without having his attention arrested by its magnificent foliage, larger than that of *R. Falconeri*, and remarkable for its brilliant deep green hue. In summer the leaves are broad, and spreading all round the plant; in winter rolled up, shrivelled, and pendulous from the tips of the branches. It is alike found at the bottom of the valleys, on the rocky spurs or slopes and ridges of the hills, in open places, or in the gloomy Pine-groves, often forming an impenetrable scrub, through which the explorer in vain seeks to force his way. Nor is this a thicket merely of twigs and foliage, that will fall under the knife or cutlass, but of thickset limbs and stout trunks, only to be severed with difficulty, on account of the toughness and unyielding nature of the wood.

The scentless blossoms expand late in April, and in May and June, but are not very copiously produced in comparison with the majority of its congeners.

Of the wood, cups, spoons, and ladles are made by the Bhoteas, and universally the little "Yak" saddle, by means of which the pack-loads are slung on the back of that animal. Easily worked, and not apt to split, it is admirably adapted for use in the parched and arid climate of Thibet. Nor is the foliage without its allotted use. The leaves are employed as platters, and serve for lining baskets for conveying the mashed pulp of *Arisæma* root (a kind of Colocass); and the accustomed present of butter or curd is always made enclosed in this glossy foliage.

Such are the characteristics of this Rhododendron, which I desire to dedicate to my excellent friend and generous host, B. H. Hodgson, Esq., of Darjeeling, formerly the Hon. East India Company's Resident at the Court of Nepal; a gentleman whose researches in the physical geography, the natural history, especially the zoology, the ethnology, the literature of the people, &c. &c., of Eastern Himalaya, are beyond all praise.

TAB. XV. *Rhododendron Hodgsoni.* Fig. 1. Flower:—*natural size.* 2. Stamen. 3. Pistil. 4. Section of ovary:—*magnified.* 5. Capsule:—*natural size.* 6. Seed with its aril. 7. Seed deprived of its aril. 8. Vertical section of a seed:—*magnified.*

J. D. H. del. Fitch, lith.

Frederic Reeve imp.

RHODODENDRON LANATUM, Hook. fil.

17.

RHODODENDRON LANATUM, *Hook. fil.*

Woolly Rhododendron.

TAB. XVI.

Arbuscula ramosa, cortice rugoso, ramis tortis, ramulis petiolis pedunculis foliisque subter lana molli subappressa albida vel fulva dense tectis, foliis elliptico-obovatis oblongisve coriaceis brevi-petiolatis apice rotundatis apiculatis basi acutis supra (costa basinque versus lanatis exceptis) glabratis subter lana molli appressa sordide albis v. fulvis, corymbo terminali capitato plurifloro, calyce minuto 5-lobo, corollæ ochroleucæ tubo lato-campanulato intus superne rubro irrorato, limbi lobis 5 rotundatis patentibus integerrimis, staminibus inclusis, filamentis basi lanatis, ovario tomentoso 5-loculari, capsula cylindracea curvata obtusa ferrugineo-floccosa.

HAB. Sikkim-Himalaya; on the rocky spurs of the humid mountains and gullies; elev. 10–12,000 feet, most common at Jongri and Chola. *Fl.* June; *fr.* November.

A large *shrub* or small *tree*, with the *trunk* six inches in diameter in the stoutest part, irregularly and repeatedly branching; *branches* much gnarled and bare of leaves, covered with a dark-coloured rugged bark, very different from the prevailing beautiful papery clothing of the genus: where it breaks off from the younger branches, however, it exposes a delicate pink liber as shown in our figure, whilst the ultimate ramuli are densely clothed with a soft appressed cottony *tomentum*. The *latter*, generally of a white or tawny colour, is uniformly spread over the petioles, peduncles, ovarium, and the whole under surface of the leaf, also extending to the upper surface of the latter, along the costa, and to the very base in a less degree. These leaves are confined to the apices of the branches, three and a half to five inches long by about two inches broad, obovate or elliptical, obtuse, with a short mucro, the base rather acute, or at most obtuse (not cordate), the colour a full yellowish-green. *Petioles* short, thick, very woolly. *Corymbs* terminal, of several, 6–10, rather large, inclined flowers. *Peduncles* an inch and a half long, thickened. *Calyx* small, reduced to five very minute blunt teeth at the top of the peduncle. *Corolla* ochroleucous or pale sulphur-colour: the *tube* broad-campanulate (like that of *R. Wightii*) within, above, and three of the upper *lobes* in part sprinkled with red dots; *limb* two inches to two and a half across, of five nearly equal, very spreading, rounded, entire obtuse *lobes*. *Stamens* ten, included: *filaments* slender, slightly curved, downy at the base; *anthers* dark brown. *Ovary* oblong-oval, furrowed, thickly woolly, five-celled. *Capsules* more than an inch long, cylindrical, curved, woolly, obtuse.

In the dense tomentum on the underside of the leaves, this species may be compared with *R. fulgens* and *R. æruginosum* among the large shrubby kinds, and with *R. Edgeworthii* and *R. pendulum* among others.

TAB. XVI. *Rhododendron lanatum.* Fig. 1. Stamen. 2. Pistil. 3. Transverse section of ovary:—*magnified.* 4. Capsule:—*natural size.*

Tab. XVII.

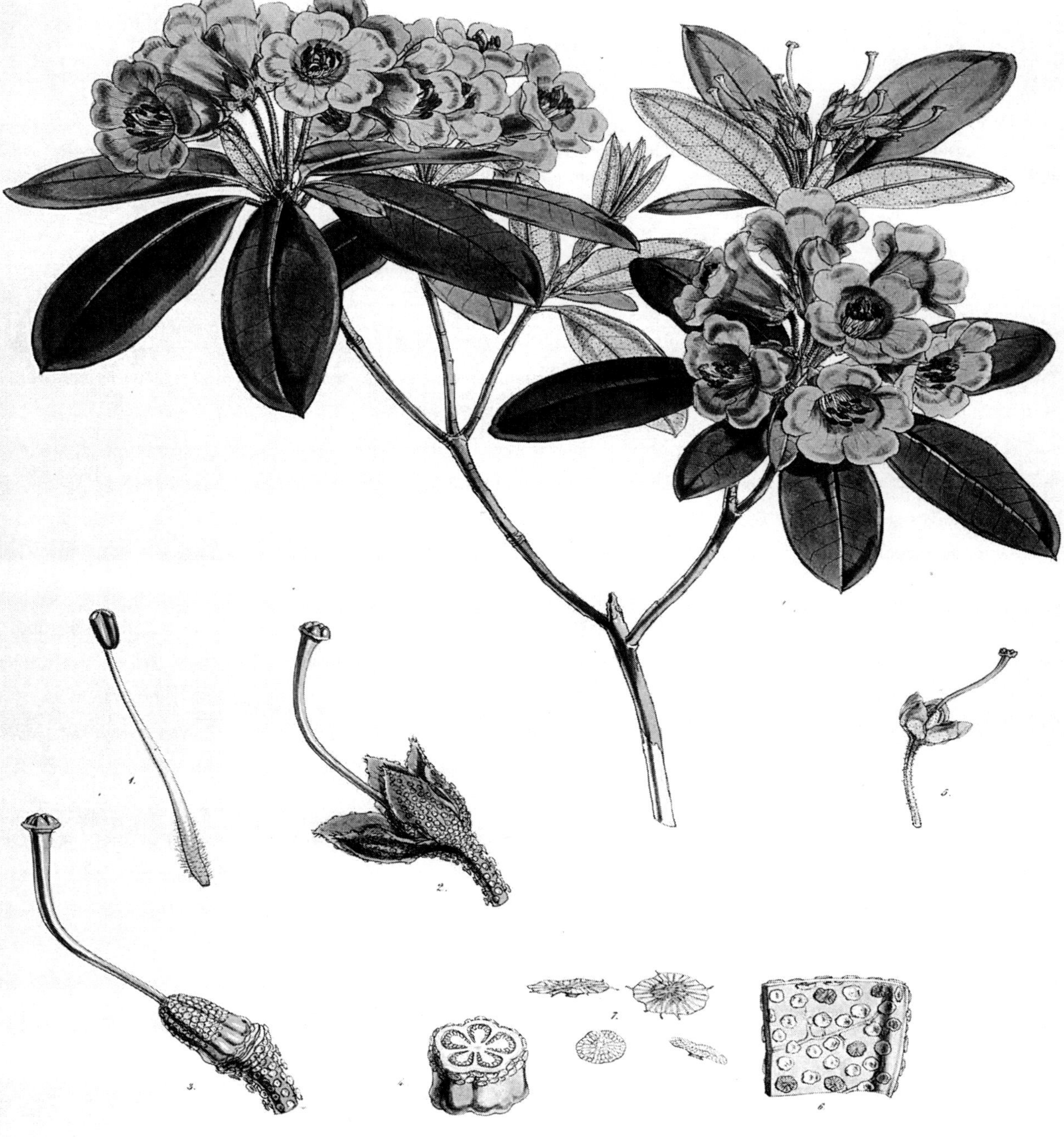

J. D. H. del. Fitch lith.

Frederic Reeve imp.

RHODODENDRON GLAUCUM, Hook. fil.

18.

RHODODENDRON GLAUCUM, *Hook. fil.*

Glaucous-leaved Rhododendron.

TAB. XVII.

Fruticulus erectus ramosus, ramulis petiolis pedunculis foliisque subtus lepidotis, foliis ellipticis seu elliptico-lanceolatis mucronatis in petiolum brevem angustatis superne denudatis subtus albo-glaucescentibus, corymbis terminalibus 6–8-floris, floribus suberectis mediocribus, calycis 5-partiti lobis ovatis acutis subfoliaceis, corollæ minute glanduloso-punctatæ roseæ tubo late campanulato intus basi pubescente, limbi lobis patentibus rotundatis emarginatis, staminibus 10, filamentis basi puberulis, ovario dense squamuloso inferne nudo, capsula subglobosa calycem persistentem æquante squamulosa glauca 5-loculari.

HAB. Sikkim-Himalaya; rocky depressed ridges of Chola, Lachen, and Lachoong; elev. 10–12,000. *Fl.* May; *fr.* November.

This constitutes a small *shrub* of the average height of two feet. *Branches* scarcely so thick as a goose-quill, yellowish-brown, often glaucous-white, the younger ones squamulose. *Leaves* rather crowded at the extremities of the branches, 1–3 inches long, usually 1–1½ inch broad, on short petioles, oblong or broadly lanceolate, obtuse, with a mucro, upper side deep green, when old naked above, below remarkably glaucous, almost white, and quite dotted with copious little scales, which in the young state covered the whole leaf, and at all times abound on the bracteas, buds, peduncles, and especially on the calyx-segments. *Peduncles* seven to eight almost in an umbel at the apices of the branches, erect, an inch or more long, rather slender. *Flowers* erect or inclined, pale pinkish-purple. *Calyx* deeply five-partite, the lobes ovate, acute, leafy, almost the length of the tube of the corolla. *Corolla* rather more than an inch long, and about as broad in the widest part: *tube* campanulate; *limb* moderately spreading, of five nearly equal rounded emarginate *lobes*. *Stamens* ten, included: *filaments* downy at the base. *Ovary* ovate, five-furrowed, upper half densely scaly. *Capsule* short, subglobose, acute, five-valved, scaly, included in the large loose persistent calyx, the valves glaucous, lepidote.

The remarkably glaucous colour* of the underside of the leaves, and the great development of the calyx, will readily distinguish this species from every other. In foliage, indeed, it has the closest resemblance to *R. virgatum*: but in that alone,—the inflorescence and calyx are widely different. The whole plant has a powerful resinous smell, due to exceedingly minute globules of a pale yellow colour, which may be seen to exude from beneath the little scales on the underside of the leaves, and which, in this species, too, abound so much on the other parts of the plant.

These scales, themselves, are very curious on the underside of the leaves of this plant: they are of two kinds; the majority are smaller, pale-coloured, exhibiting several concentric circles of minute, nearly uniform cells; the larger ones are setose at the margin, and consist of a centre or disc of small cells, while the circumference forms a limb or margin of radiating elongated cells (see fig. 6, 7).

* This glaucous hue is fully retained in the well-dried specimens, but disappears from those that have been by any accident wetted.

TAB. XVII. *Rhododendron glaucum.* Fig. 1. Stamen. 2. Calyx and pistil. 3. Pistil. 4. Transverse section of the ovary:—*magnified.* 5. Fruit included in the calyx, and with the persistent style:—*natural size.* 6. Portion of a young leaf, showing the scales:—*magnified.* 7. Exhibits the two different scales separated from the leaf:—*more highly magnified.*

Tab. XVIII

J. H. D. del. Fitch, lith.

Reeve & Nichols, imp.

RHODODENDRON MADDENI, Hook. fil.

19.

RHODODENDRON MADDENI, *Hook. fil.*

Major Madden's Rhododendron.

TAB. XVIII.

Frutex erectus virgatus, ramulis pedunculis petiolis foliisque subter ferrugineo-lepidotis, foliis petiolatis elliptico-lanceolatis utrinque acutis acuminatisve marginibus planis superne nitidis viridibus, pedunculis 2–3 terminalibus brevibus crassis, calycis brevis 5-fidi lobis inæqualibus supremo nunc elongato, corolla extus lepidota ampla, tubo contracto elongato, limbi patentissimi lobis maximis rotundis integris, staminibus 18–20, filamentis glaberrimis, stylo longissimo ovarioque lepidotis, capsula elliptica 10-loculari lignosa.

HAB. Sikkim-Himalaya; inner ranges, very rare: in thickets by the Lachen and Lachoong rivers at Choongtam; elev. 6,000 feet. *Fl.* June to August; *fr.* November.

A *shrub* six to eight feet high, branching from the base. *Branches* erect, supple, covered with pale, papery *bark*. *Leaves* abundant, very bright green, of a coriaceous substance but flaccid, elliptical-lanceolate, acute or acuminate, gradually tapering below into the rather short ferruginous petiole, 4–7 inches long, frequently pendulous; the young ones entirely, the perfect ones beneath only, or sometimes partially above, clothed with dense, white squamules, which become ferruginous in age, the costa below eventually losing them. *Peduncles* about three, short, stout, lepidote. *Calyx* (as in *R. Roylei*) variable in form, always small in proportion to the size of the flower, somewhat membranous at the margin, five-lobed, the lobes obtuse, the upper one generally much prolonged. *Corolla* three and a half to four inches long, and as much across the limb, very handsome, pure white, with a faint blush, chiefly on the upper lobe, rather fleshy, but firm, in substance, the *tube* sparingly lepidote, in shape rather infundibuliform than campanulate, being so much more contracted than is usual with the Himalayan species; the *limb* very large, spreading, of five, nearly equal, rounded, entire *lobes*, slightly crenato-undulate at the margin, delicately but obscurely veined. *Stamens* eighteen to twenty, as long as the tube: *filaments* very slender, glabrous; *anthers* ochreous-yellow. *Ovary* small for the size of the flower, ten-celled, elliptical, whitish with the copious squamules. *Style* very long, exserted much beyond the stamens and the mouth of the corolla, thickened upwards, lepidote. *Stigma* large, often morbidly incrassate and lobulate. *Capsule* oval-oblong, cylindrical, short, straight, obtuse at both ends, about an inch and a quarter long, and half that in breadth.

Of this species the foliage and the flowers are faintly odorous. Very different as this may appear at first sight from *R. cinnabarinum* (Tab. VII. of this work), it clearly belongs to the same natural groupe along with *R. Roylei*. The very large white flowers, the numerous stamens, and ten-celled fruit abundantly distinguish it.

I do myself the pleasure to name this truly superb plant in compliment to Major Madden of the Bengal Civil Service, a good and accomplished botanist, to whose learned memoirs on the plants of the temperate and tropical zones of North-west Himalaya, the reader may be referred for an excellent account of the vegetation of those regions. The same gentleman's paper on the *Coniferæ* of the north of India may be quoted as a model of its kind.

TAB. XVIII. *Rhododendron Maddeni.* Fig. 1. Stamen. 2. Calyx and pistil. 3. Transverse section of ovary:—*magnified.* 4. Capsule:—*natural size.* 5. Portion of the lepidote underside of a leaf:—*magnified.*

Tab. XIX.

J. D. H. del. Fitch, lith.

Reeve & Nichols, imp.

RHODODENDRON TRIFLORUM, Hook. fil.

20.

RHODODENDRON TRIFLORUM, *Hook. fil.*

Three-flowered Rhododendron.

TAB. XIX.

Frutex erectus, ramulis glaucescentibus novellis petiolis pedunculis foliisque subtus creberrime lepidotis, foliis ovato-lanceolatis utrinque acutis v. basi subcordatis superne nitidis subtus glaucis vel subferrugineis, pedunculis sub-3 terminalibus gracilibus, calyce brevi 5-lobato lepidoto ciliato, corollæ flavidæ tubo brevi obconico dorso minute lepidoto lobis oblongis patentibus integris, staminibus 8–10, filamentis elongatis inferne villosis, ovario 5-loculari oblongo lepidoto, stylo elongato, stigmate truncato, capsula oblonga, valvis lignosis.

HAB. Sikkim-Himalaya; inner ranges, on brushy slopes; elev. 7–9,000 feet; scarce. *Fl.* May, June; *fr.* November.

A *shrub* four to six feet high, with erect and rather twiggy *branches* for the genus, the ultimate ones about as thick as a duck's quill: the new shoots lepidote. *Leaves* frequently pendulous, on rather short slender *petioles* (one-third of an inch long), ovato-lanceolate, more or less approaching to oblong or elliptical, two or rarely three inches long, acute at both ends, or cordate at the base and sometimes blunt, with a mucro at the apex, the margin a little recurved, substance rather thin, upper surface smooth and shining, under quite glabrous and glaucous, but so beset with *ferruginous* squamules as to partake of that colour. *Peduncles* generally three together, terminal one-half to three-fourths of an inch long, slender, erect. *Calyx* very short, lepidote, cut into five small rounded teeth or lobes. *Corolla* greenish-yellow, in shape much resembling that of the common garden Azaleas, having a somewhat obconical tube very open at the mouth, and a limb of five spreading oblong entire segments, which are slightly veiny, nearly two inches across the lobes. *Stamens* eight, much exserted: *filaments* slender, hairy near the base. *Ovary* oblong-cylindrical, very lepidote, obtuse. *Style* much longer than the stamens, curved upwards, and terminating in a truncated *stigma*, a little thickened in the disc. *Capsule* half an inch long, straight, cylindrical, often a little swollen at the base, obtuse at the point.

The present *Rhododendron* will form a groupe or section along with *R. virgatum*, Hook. fil., *R. setosum*, Don, and *R. nivale*, Hook. fil.; all of which have peculiarly narrow segments to the corolla. But the present species is well distinguished by its comparatively large yellow flowers, and the larger, usually pointed, leaves.

TAB. XIX. Fig. 1. Stamen. 2. Calyx and pistil. 3. Transverse section of ovary. 4. Small lepidote portion of the underside of the leaf:—*magnified*. 5. Squamules from the leaf:—*more magnified*.

J. D. H. del. Fitch, lith.

Reeve & Nichols, imp.

RHODODENDRON SETOSUM, Wall.

21.

RHODODENDRON SETOSUM, *Don.*

Bristly Rhododendron.

Tab. XX.

Fruticulus humilis ramosissimus, ramulis setosis foliis utrinque pedunculis calycibusque creberrime lepidotis, foliis parvis brevissime petiolatis (petiolo setoso) ellipticis subovatisve marginibus subrecurvis ciliatis læte viridibus subtus glaucis v. pallide ferrugineis, pedunculis 3–5 terminalibus brevibus, calycis lobis subfoliaceis ovalibus obtusis coloratis, corollæ purpureo-roseæ tubo brevissimo lobis 5 oblongis obtusis integris patentibus, staminibus 8–10 exsertis, filamentis basim versus barbatis, ovario brevi lepidoto, stylo superne incrassato capsula calycem persistentem æquante brevi crassa lepidota 5-loculari.

Rhododendron setosum, *Don, Wern. Trans.* vol. iii. p. 408. *Prodr. Fl. Nep.* p. 152. *De Cand. Prodr.* vol. vii. p. 784.

Hab. Gossain-Than. *Hamilton, Wallich* in Herb. nostr. Sikkim-Himalaya; open stony and rocky places, abundant; elev. 13–16,000 feet. *Fl.* June, July; *fr.* October.

Stems from a span to a foot high, much and repeatedly branched, *branches* sometimes verticillate, covered with a papery bark, the youngest ones setose and very lepidote, which last character extends to both sides of the leaves, peduncles, calyx, and ovary. *Leaves* small, copious towards the ends of the branches, one-third to half an inch long, elliptical or obovate, coriaceous, very obtuse, dark green above, pale and glaucous beneath, setose on the recurved margin; *petiole* short, setose. *Peduncles* half an inch to one inch long, three to five from the ends of the numerous branches, very lepidote, erect. *Flowers* inclined. *Calyx* coloured, red, large for the size of the corolla, deeply cut into five oval very obtuse foliaceous lobes, very squamulose at the back and edge, nearly naked towards the margin. *Corolla* bright red-rose colour, an inch and a half across, five-partite, the tube very short: the *lobes* spreading, oblong, waved, and sinuated at the margin. *Stamens* eight to ten, much exserted: *filaments* slender, with a dense tuft of hairs above the base; *anthers* oblong. *Ovary* ovate, obtuse, very squamulose, five-celled. *Style* long, ascending, thickened upwards: *stigma* a depressed disc, bearing five prominent *points* or *lobes*. *Capsule* a quarter of an inch long, subglobose, densely lepidote, enclosed by the persistent calyx.

A small and elegant shrub, with a good deal the aspect of *Rhodora*, especially in the flowers, but these are more copious and brighter coloured, and the foliage is Box-like and evergreen. It is the "*Tsallu*" of the Sikkim-Bhoteas and Thibetians, who attribute the oppression and headaches attending the crossing of the loftiest passes of Eastern Himalaya, to the strongly resinous odour of this and of the *Rhododendron anthopogon*, Wall. ("*Palu*" of the natives). The species certainly abounds to within a few miles of the summits of all the passes, and, after hot sunshine, fills the atmosphere with its powerful aroma, too heavy by far to be agreeable; and it is indeed a sad aggravation to the discomforts of toiling in the rarified medium it inhabits. Covering, as it does, extensive moorland tracts and rocky slopes, the brilliant red purple of its flowers renders it a charming and most lovely object. In its late flowering (June and July) and early fruiting (October) it is eminently typical of the briefer and more distinctly circumscribed summer of those elevated regions:—and no less so are its powerfully strong odour and copious resinous secretions of a drier climate than any, except a very few of its congeners, enjoy. The hand, on being passed over the foliage and branches, is imbued with the clammy exudation, and which long retains the scent. An useful volatile oil, of no less marked character than that of the American *Gaultheria* * (now in great demand by the perfumers) would probably be yielded by distillation of the foliage.

* *Gaultheria procumbens,* which yields the "*Oil of Wintergreen,*" used by perfumers and by druggists to flavour syrups.

Tab. XX. *Rhododendron setosum.* Fig. 1. Stamen. 2. Calyx and pistil. 3. Transverse section of ovary. 4. Upper, and 5, underside of a leaf, with a portion of the branch. 6. Scales from the leaf:—*all more or less magnified.*

THE

RHODODENDRONS

OF

SIKKIM-HIMALAYA;

BEING

AN ACCOUNT, BOTANICAL AND GEOGRAPHICAL, OF THE
RHODODENDRONS RECENTLY DISCOVERED IN THE MOUNTAINS OF EASTERN HIMALAYA,

FROM

DRAWINGS AND DESCRIPTIONS MADE ON THE SPOT,

DURING A GOVERNMENT BOTANICAL MISSION TO THAT COUNTRY;

BY

JOSEPH DALTON HOOKER, R.N., M.D., F.R.S., F.L.S.,

&c., &c., &c.

EDITED BY

SIR W. J. HOOKER, K.H., D.C.L., F.R.S., F.L.S., &c.

Vice-President of the Linnean Society, and Director of the Royal Gardens of Kew.

PART III.

LONDON:
REEVE AND BENHAM, HENRIETTA STREET, COVENT GARDEN.

1851.

Tab. XXI

J. D. H. del. Fitch. lith.

Reeve & Nichols imp.

RHODODENDRON EDGEWORTHI, Hook. fil.

RHODODENDRON EDGEWORTHII, *Hook. fil.*

Mr. Edgeworth's Rhododendron.

TAB. XXI.

Frutex sæpe epiphytus, ramulis petiolis pedunculis capsulis foliisque subtus dense ferrugineo-villoso-tomentosis, foliis sublonge petiolatis elliptico-ovatis acutis vel acuminatis subcoriaceis rugoso-reticulatis basi obtusis supra nitidis marginibus recurvis, pedunculis 2–3 terminalibus v. ab innovationibus lateralibus, floribus speciosis albis, calycis ampli 5-partiti lobis foliaceis oblongo-obovatis inæqualibus lanuginosis ciliatis, corollæ tubo breviusculo late campanulato, limbi maximi lobis rotundatis venosis crenato-undulatis, staminibus 10 exsertis, filamentis inferne villosis, antheris elongatis, ovario dense tomentoso 5-loculari, stylo gracili basi lanuginoso, capsula oblongo-cylindracea recta obtusa valvis lignosis.

HAB. Sikkim-Himalaya; in valleys of the inner ranges, usually pendulous from trees, sometimes on rocks; elevation 7,000–9,000 feet. *Fl.* May and June; *fr.* November.

A small *shrub*, with straggling branches, often pendulous upon trees and rocks. *Branches*, the older ones covered with a dark ashy and slightly glaucous bark; young ones and young leaves and bracts, peduncles, petioles, and the underside of the old leaves, densely clothed with a soft ferrugineo-fulvous tomentum, which is easily detached. *Leaves* two to four inches long, ovato-lanceolate, acute or more usually suddenly acuminate, obtuse at the base, the margin recurved, the upper surface fine glossy green, singularly rugose from the deeply impressed reticulated veins; beneath, too, the principal veins are prominent and conspicuous. *Petioles* about three-quarters of an inch long. *Peduncles* terminal or axillary from innovations, usually two or three from the same point, about as long as the petioles. *Flowers* very large, showy, inclined. *Calyx* large, of five deep, membranaceous or foliaceous, obovate, spreading, unequal, coloured lobes, very downy on the back, the edges finely ciliated. *Corolla* white, often tinged with blush and pale yellow: the *tube* rather short, widening much at the mouth, slightly curved, the *limb* unusually large, more than four inches across, spreading, of five nearly equal, rounded, slightly emarginate lobes, crisped at the margin, delicately veined on the surface. *Stamens* ten, a good deal exserted beyond the mouth of the tube: *filaments* slender, a little dilated downwards, villous on the lower half: *anthers* very large, long in proportion to their breadth, linear-oblong, dark purple-brown. *Ovary* ovoid, six-furrowed, six-celled, densely woolly: *style* elongated, red, woolly below: *stigma* five- to six-lobed. *Capsule* more than an inch long, straight, oblong-cylindrical, obtuse, densely covered with ferruginous wool. *Seeds* pale-coloured.

A truly superb species from the size of the flowers and their roseate tinge on a white ground, also on account of the variety of rich colour in the leaves, bracteas, stipules, calyx, &c., while the very wrinkled surface of the leaf adds much to its beauty. In its floccose character and foliaceous calyx it resembles *R. pendulum*; but in the size and shape of the flowers it approaches *R. Dalhousiæ*, next to which I would place it.

The majority of my specimens were obtained from the land-shoots, or -slips, in the rocky ravines, which bring down in their course those Pines on the limbs of which this species delights to grow.

I dedicate this Rhododendron to my accomplished and excellent friend, M. P. Edgeworth, Esq., of the Bengal Civil Service, now Commissioner of Mooltan, who has long and successfully studied the Botany of Western Himalaya, and of North-western India generally.

TAB. XXI. *Rhododendron Edgeworthii.* Fig. 1. Stamen. 2. Calyx and pistil. 3. Transverse section of ovary:—*magnified.* 4. Pistil with its persistent calyx:—*natural size.*

Tab. XXII.

J.D.H. del. Fitch lith.

Reeve & Nichols, imp.

RHODODENDRON ÆRUGINOSUM. Hook. fil.

23.

RHODODENDRON ÆRUGINOSUM, *Hook. fil.*

Æruginose Rhododendron.

TAB. XXII.

Frutex densissime racemosus, ramis cortice papyraceo tectis, ramulis petiolis pedunculis foliisque superne glaberrimis, foliis petiolatis obovatis obovato-oblongisve apice acutis v. muticis basi cordatis subtus dense ferrugineo-tomentosis, capitulo conferto vix densifloro, floribus lilacinis v. roseis, pedicellis subelongatis, calyce breve 5-dentato, corolla campanulata basi intus plaga sanguinea v. lobo superiore tantum maculato, staminibus 10, antheris majusculis, filamentis glabris, ovario glaberrimo 5–8-loculari, capsulis cylindraceis elongatis.

HAB. Sikkim-Himalaya, growing with *Rhododendron fulgens*, and equally abundant, flowering at the same season.

The colour of the flower, the loose capitulum, long pedicels, and campanulate corolla, distinguish this species from *R. fulgens*; in the fruiting season, too, its longer, more slender capsules afford a marked character, as does the more evidently toothed calyx. When dried, however, they are so difficult to discriminate, that I have felt inclined to unite them. The leaves are identical in all respects, except that those of this species have a remarkable verdigris hue. It is still more closely allied to *R. campanulatum*. Of all the Sikkim shrubby Rhododendrons of any size, these two attain the highest level, reaching nearly to 15,000 feet in the remote Lachoong valley, and 14,000 feet in that of the Lachen: 13,000 is their usual level in the ascending zone.

TAB. XXII. *Rhododendron æruginosum*. Fig. 1. Stamen. 2. Peduncle, calyx, and pistil. 3. Transverse section of ovarium:—*all magnified*. 4. Fruit:—*natural size*.

Tab. XXIII

J.D.H. del. Fitch, lith.

Reeve & Nichols, imp.

RHODODENDRON SALIGNUM, Hook.fil. | RHODODENDRON ELÆAGNOIDES, Hook.fil.

24.

RHODODENDRON SALIGNUM, *Hook. fil.*

Willow-leaved Rhododendron.

TAB. XXIII. A.

Fruticulus erectus, ramis erectis apice fasciculatim ramulosis, ramulis foliis utrinque pedunculo calyce corollaque extus creberrime squamuloso-lepidotis, foliis breve petiolatis patulis pendulisve elliptico- v. lineari-lanceolatis utrinque acuminatis subtus pallidioribus, pedicellis solitariis v. 2–3 elongatis gracilibus erectis, calycis lobis patulis obtusis subfoliaceis, corolla lutea v. viridi-sulphurea, tubo inflato brevi, limbi lobis patulis v. recurvis orbicularibus 3 superioribus viridi-maculatis, staminibus 8–10 exsertis, stylo crasso curvo, ovario brevi albo-lepidoto 5-loculari.

HAB. Sikkim-Himalaya; grassy and rocky hills above Choongtam, elev. 7,000 feet; common. *Fl.* May, June.

A slender twiggy *shrub*, two to four feet high, branching from a stout tortuous stock; the *branches* as thick as a crow-quill, rather scattered, bearing fascicled ramuli at the top. *Leaves* often drooping, rather flaccid, of a pale glaucous green, lighter underneath and sometimes ferruginous where the lepidote scales abound, an inch to an inch and a half long, scarcely half an inch broad, acute or mucronate. *Pedicels* always elongated, an inch and a half to two inches long, slender. *Corolla* yellow, an inch across the lobes, lepidote, especially on the outside of the tube; the upper lobes are spotted with green, the spots occupying the spaces between the very broad anastomosing translucent veins. *Anthers* large, rich red-brown; *filaments* short, stout, villous below. *Ovarium* covered with white lepidote squamulæ. *Stigma* very stout, curved, gradually thickened towards the truncated stigmatiferous apex. *Capsules* not seen.

The odour of this plant is strongly resinous. As a species it is very closely allied to the *R. lepidotum*; but the leaves are much longer, and the pedicels always elongated; characters by no means satisfactory. *R. elæagnoides* may prove another state of the same species.

TAB. XXIII. A. *Rhododendron salignum.* Fig. 1. Plant:—*natural size.* 2. Stamen. 3. Peduncle, calyx, and pistil. 4. Portion of under surface of leaf:—*all magnified.*

25.

RHODODENDRON ELÆAGNOIDES, *Hook. fil.*

Oleaster-leaved Rhododendron.

TAB. XXIII. B.

Fruticulus humilis, nunc depressus, ramosissimus, more *Ericæ* gregarius, ramulis scabridis ultimis apice foliiferis, foliis pedicellis calyce corolla extus ovarioque dense lepidotis, squamulis ferrugineis argenteisque, foliis verticillatim confertis breviter petiolatis late obovatis obcordatisve retusis obtusisve mucronatis, pedicellis terminalibus solitariis rarius binis elongatis erectis, calycis lobis foliaceis patulis recurvisve rufescentibus, corolla flava pro planta ampla, tubo brevi basi globoso, limbi lobis patulis concavis 3 supremis obscure maculatis, staminibus 8–10, filamentis basi villosis, antheris majusculis, ovario brevi 5-lobo dense lepidoto, stylo crasso decurvo, capsulis parvis.

HAB. Sikkim-Himalaya; open rocky places, elev. 12–16,000 feet; most abundant. *Fl.* June and July.

Undoubtedly the smallest species of this section, growing in widely extended clumps, much as heather does, but never so extensively, emitting in sunshine a powerful resinous odour. *Leaves* fasciculated at the apices of the ramuli, generally spreading in a rotate manner, pale yellowish-green, very copiously covered with lepidote squamulæ, a quarter to half an inch long. *Pedicels* an inch to an inch and a half long. *Flowers* large for the size of the plant, of the same form as *R. salignum* and *lepidotum*, but much larger, varying from yellow (the usual colour) to deep red-purple, spotted faintly on the three upper lobes. *Stamens* generally eight. *Capsule* very small, a quarter of an inch in length, twice as long as the calyx, five-valved, five-celled. *Seeds* pale-coloured.

This and the *R. lepidotum* and *salignum* may prove extreme varieties of one species.

TAB. XXIII. *Rhododendron elæagnoides.* Figs. 1 and 2. Plants:—*natural size.* 3. Stamen. 4. Peduncle, calyx, and ovarium. 5. Transverse section of ovarium:—*all magnified.* 6. Fruit:—*natural size.*

J. D. H. del. Fitch lith.

Reeve & Nichols imp.

RHODODENDRON CILIATUM, Hook. fil.

26.

RHODODENDRON CILIATUM, *Hook. fil.*

Ciliated Rhododendron.

TAB. XXIV.

Fruticulus rigidus, erectus, caulibus plurimis validis, ramulis pedunculis pedicellisque hispido-pilosis, foliis ellipticis acuminatis coriaceis super marginibus ciliato-pilosis senioribus glabratis subtus (costa excepta) glaberrimis pallidis creberrime ferrugineo-punctatis, pedicellis validis subconfertis (2–5), calyce basi hispido, lobis late ovatis obtusis coriaceis, corolla campanulata pallide purpurea, staminibus 10, filamentis basi pilosis, stylo gracili, capsula brevi crassa calyce duplo longiore 5-loculari infra apicem contracta.

HAB. Sikkim-Himalaya, inner ranges only, in wet rocky places, rarely in woods. Lachen and Lachoong valleys; elev. 9–10,000 feet. *Fl.* May; *fr.* October.

A small very rigid *shrub*, growing in clumps two feet high, generally in moist rocky places. Odour faintly resinous and pleasant. Whole plant more or less pilose and setose, the hairs long and fulvous on the young leaves; petioles and pedicels patent. *Leaves* two, rarely three inches long, sometimes obscurely cordate at the base. Upper surface (except in age) pilose, even villous when young, underneath quite glabrous, covered with minute orbicular ferruginous scales. *Bracteas* rather membranous, ciliated. *Capitula* three- to five-flowered, terminal; pedicels very stout, one inch long; flowers inclined. *Sepals* nearly equal, membranous, veined, ciliated. *Corolla* one inch and a half long, nearly as much across at the mouth; *tube* rather contracted below, *limb* five-lobed, colour pale reddish-purple, upper lobe obscurely spotted. *Anthers* large. *Stigma* exserted, capitate. *Capsule* woody, one-third to one-half of an inch long, suddenly contracted below the apex, each of the five valves there recurved or beaked, the back covered with minute scales. *Seeds* pale-coloured.

Allied to *R. barbatum*, but widely different in stature, habit, and the scattered scales on the under surface of the leaves. I have not observed it in other valleys than those flanked by snowy mountains, where it is common, scenting the air in warm weather.

The scales (as in many of its congeners) are orbicular, sessile, and peltately attached, formed of three concentric series of cells, the outer elongated in the direction of the radius. A dark concentric line marks the union of the circumferential series of cells with those next to it. The fragrant oil is secreted chiefly in the discoid cell.

TAB. XXIV. *Rhododendron ciliatum.* Fig. 1. Stamen. 2. Peduncle, calyx, and pistil. 3. Transverse section of ovarium. 4. Fruit. 5. Under surface of portion of leaf. 6. Scales from the same:—*magnified.*

Tab. XXV.

J.D.H. del. Fitch lith. Reeve & Nichols imp.

RHODODENDRON FULGENS, Hook. fil.

27.

RHODODENDRON FULGENS, *Hook. fil.*

Brilliant Rhododendron.

TAB. XXV.

Frutex densissime ramosus, foliosus, ramis cortice papyraceo tectis, ramulis pedunculis petiolis ovariis foliisque superne glaberrimis, foliis petiolatis late obovato- v. ovato-ellipticis apice rotundatis basi cordatis margine recurvo subtus tomento flocceso ferrugineo dense vestitis, capitulis densifloris, pedicellis brevibus, calyce obsoleto v. brevissimo disciformi lobato, corolla intense sanguinea campanulata, tubo subcompresso, limbi lobis 5 rotundatis breviusculis recurvis, staminibus 10, filamentis glabris, ovario conico basi turgido apice truncato 8-loculari 8-sulcato, capsulis oblongo-cylindraceis obtusis gibbosis glaucis purpureis.

HAB. Sikkim-Himalaya; mountain slopes and spurs, elev. 12–14,000 feet; abundant. *Fl.* June; *fr.* November and December.

This, the richest ornament of the alpine region in the month of June, forms a very prevalent shrub at the elevations assigned to it, not yielding in abundance to its constant associates, *R. æruginosum* and *R. Maddeni*, and, like the former, pushing forth young leaves of a beautiful verdigris-green in July and August. The foliage is perennial, and gives a singular hue to the bleak snowy mountain-faces immediately overhung by the perpetual snow, contrasting in August in broad masses or broken clumps with the bright scarlet of the Berberry, the golden yellow of the fading Birch and Mountain Ash, the lurid heavy green of the perennial Juniper, and the bleak raw brown of the withered herbage. Whether, then, for the glorious effulgence in spring of its deep scarlet blossoms, which appear to glow like fire in the short hour of morning sunlight, or the singular tint it at other seasons wears, this is among the most striking of the plants which lend to these inhospitable regions the varied hues which are denied to the comparatively habitable but gloomy forests of the temperate zone on the same mountains.

Individual shrubs are generally of a rounded outline, about four feet high, and twice as much in diameter, and when growing together they compose an impenetrable thicket, as annoying to the traveller as *R. Hodgsoni* is at lower elevations. The ramuli are bright green, the thickness of a little finger. *Leaves* four inches long and three broad, pretty constant in form, and always coriaceous in texture, with a glossy upper surface, and dense woolly clothing underneath, which wholly obliterates the venation. *Corolla* of a deep, bright blood-red, somewhat fleshy in texture, highly polished and shining. *Anthers* dark brown; *filaments* pink. *Style* rather short, curved, ending in a truncate stigma, not materially enlarged. The *capsules* are one to two inches long, very stout, of a fine plum-purple colour, and covered with a glaucous bloom.

There is no pubescence, glands, or squamæ, on any part of the plant, except on the inner bracteal scales, which are silky, and on the very young foliage, which has often a little villous pubescence: the latter, which is wholly scentless, is not to be distinguished from that of *R. æruginosum*.

TAB. XXV. *Rhododendron fulgens.* Fig. 1. Flower. 2. Stamen. 3. Peduncle, calyx, and ovarium. 4. Transverse section of ovarium. 5. Fruit:—*all but figures* 1 *and* 5 *magnified.*

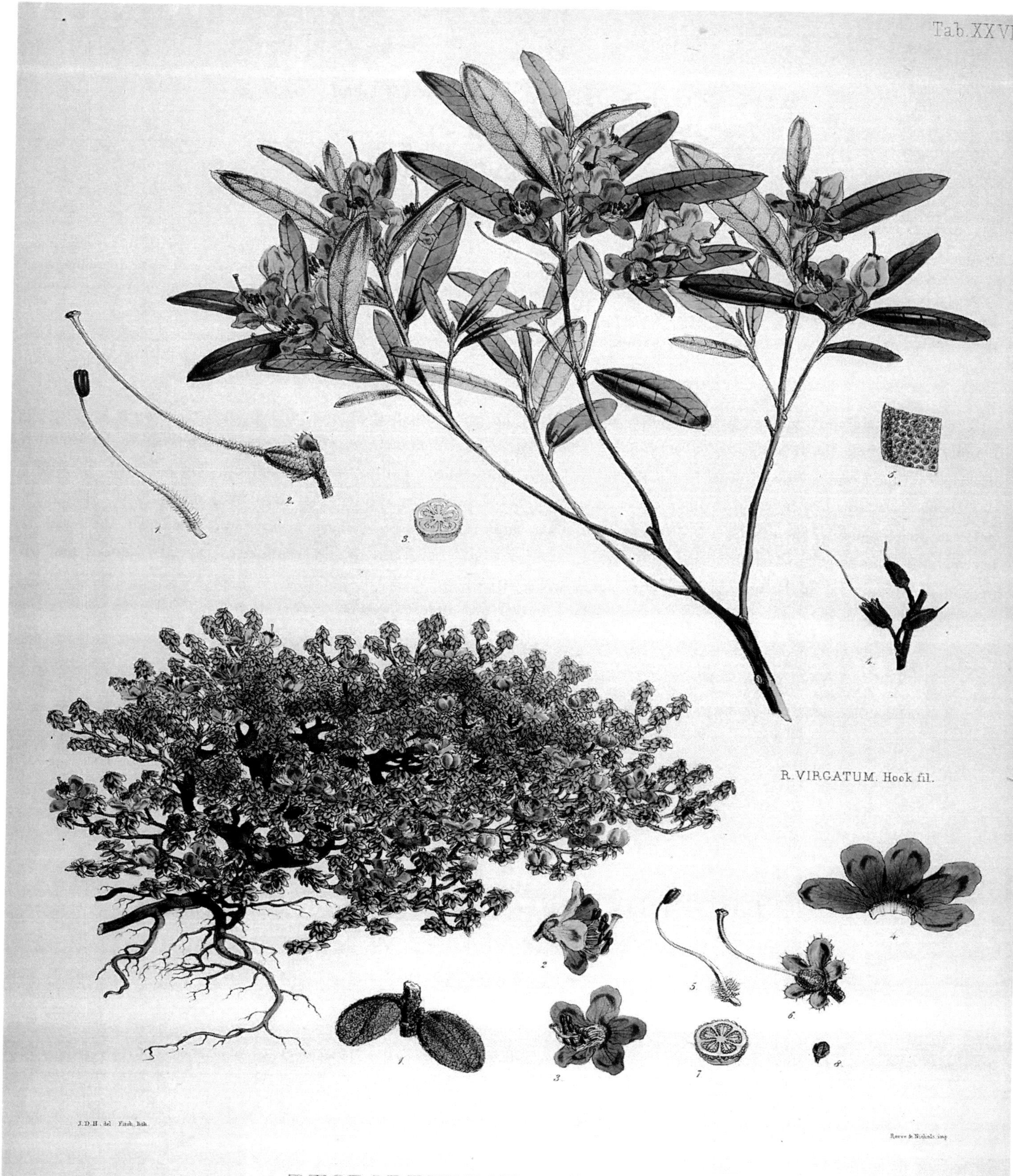

RHODODENDRON NIVALE, Hook.fil.

28.

RHODODENDRON VIRGATUM, *Hook. fil.*

Twiggy Rhododendron.

TAB. XXVI. A.

Fruticulus gracilis, erectus, virgatus, ramulis pedicellis foliisque squamulosis, foliis lineari-ellipticis lanceolatisve mucronatis subtus albo-glaucescentibus vel pallidioribus, pedicellis brevibus axillaribus solitariis rarius binis, bracteis chartaceis concavis suffultis, calyce abbreviato obtuse 5-lobo, corolla campanulata glanduloso-punctata, tubo subcontracto, lobis angustis, staminibus 8–10, filamentis basi lanatis, stigmate exserto capitato, capsula 5-loculari ovata vel breviter cylindracea squamulis ferrugineis tecta, seminibus pallidis.

HAB. Sikkim-Himalaya; skirts of Pine-forests in ravines, elev. 8–9,000 feet. Lachen valley. *Fl.* May; *fr.* October.

Decidedly the most slender twiggy species with which I am acquainted, the stems and branches reaching four feet in height, and scarcely the thickness of a crow-quill. The *leaves* are so like those of *R. glaucum* as to require no detailed description. *Flowers* solitary, rarely in pairs, and axillary: the pedicels two to three lines long, covered with sheathing deciduous coriaceous brown scales, which are longer than the pedicel, very rigid in texture, downy on the back. *Corolla* a pale red-purple, smaller than that of *R. triflorum*, but of the same form: the *tube* short, narrow and obconical, the *segments* narrow and spreading. *Style* long; *stigma* exserted. *Calycine lobes* short, broad and rounded. *Capsules* seldom half an inch long, surrounded at the base by the short appressed calyx.

The axillary flowers and nature of the imbricating bracts are almost peculiar to this species.

TAB. XXVI. A. *Rhododendron virgatum.* Fig. 1. Stamen. 2. Calyx and pistil. 3. Transverse section of ovarium. 4. Fruit. 5. Portion of under surface of leaf:—*all but fig. 4 magnified.*

29.

RHODODENDRON NIVALE, *Hook. fil.*

Snow Rhododendron.

TAB. XXVI. B.

Fruticulus depressus, prostratus, ramosissimus, ramis ramulisque tortis cortice fusco tectis, foliis minimis terminalibus confertis patulis ramulisque dense ferrugineo-lepidotis, petiolo brevissimo, lamina coriacea elliptico-oblonga obovatave utrinque obtusa, marginibus subrecurvis subtus glaucescentibus, pedicellis solitariis terminalibus brevissimis, calyce laxe lepidoto, lobis submembranaceis ciliatis, corolla parva (rubro-purpurea), tubo brevissimo, lobis oblongis lineari-oblongisve obtusis patulis, staminibus 8–10 exsertis, antheris oblongis majusculis, filamentis gracilibus basi villosis, ovario densissime lepidoto, stylo gracili, stigmate capitato, capsula calyce longiore brevissime obovata 5-valvi.

HAB. Sikkim-Himalaya; on the loftiest bare slopes of the mountains on the Thibetan frontier, elev. 16–18,000 feet. *Fl.* June and July; *fr.* September and October.

The hard woody branches of this curious little species, as thick as a goose-quill, straggle along the ground for a foot or two, presenting brown tufts of vegetation where not half a dozen other plants can exist. The branches are densely interwoven, very harsh and woody, wholly depressed; whence the shrub, spreading horizontally, and barely raised two inches above the soil, becomes eminently typical of the arid stern climate it inhabits. The latest to bloom and earliest to mature its seeds, by far the smallest in foliage, and proportionally largest in flower, most lepidote in vesture, humble in stature, rigid in texture, deformed in habit, yet the most odoriferous, it may be recognized, even in the herbarium, as the production of the loftiest elevation on the surface of the globe,—of the most excessive climate,—of the joint influences of a scorching sun by day, and the keenest frost at night,—of the greatest drought followed in a few hours by a saturated atmosphere,—of the balmiest calm alternating with the whirlwind of the Alps. For eight months of the year it is buried under many feet of snow: for the remaining four it is frequently snowed and sunned in the same hour. During genial weather, when the sun heats the soil to 150°, its perfumed foliage scents the air; whilst to snow-storm and frost it is insensible, blooming through all, expanding its little purple flowers to the day, and only closing them to wither after fertilization has taken place. As the life of a moth may be indefinitely prolonged, whilst its duties are unfulfilled, so the flower of this little mountaineer will remain open through days of fog and sleet, till a mild day facilitates the detachment of the pollen and fecundation of the ovarium. This process is almost wholly the effect of the winds; for though humble-bees, and the "Blues" and "Fritillaries" (*Polyommatus* and *Argynnis*) amongst butterflies, do exist at the same prodigious elevation, they are too few in number to influence the operations of vegetable life.

The odour of the plant much resembles that of "Eau de Cologne." Lepidote *scales* generally rather a bright ferruginous-brown, wholly concealing the ramuli, foliage, &c. *Leaves* one-eighth to one-sixth of an inch long, pale green. *Corolla* one-third of an inch across the lobes. The nearest allies of this species are *R. setosum* and *R. Lapponicum*, from which latter it differs in its smaller stature and solitary sessile flowers.

This singular little plant attains a loftier elevation, I believe, than any other shrub in the world.

TAB. XXVI. B. *Rhododendron nivale.* Fig. 1. Branch and leaves. 2 and 3. Flowers. 4. Corolla laid open. 5. Stamen. 6. Calyx and pistil. 7. Transverse section of ovarium:—*all magnified.* 8. Fruit:—*natural size.*

Tab. XXVII.

J. D. H. del. Fitch lith.

Reeve & Nichols, imp.

RHODODENDRON WIGHTII. Hook fil.

30.

RHODODENDRON WIGHTII, *Hook. fil.*

Dr. Wight's Rhododendron.

TAB. XXVII.

Arbuscula ramosa, ramis cortice papyraceo tectis, foliis lanceolatis elliptico-lanceolatisve utrinque acutis superne glaberrimis subtus lana arctissime appressa rufa tectis marginibus planis, petiolo puberulo, capitulis multifloris, bracteis coriaceis glaberrimis viscidis, pedicellis gracilibus puberulis, calyce obsoleto, corolla ampla campanulata pallide straminea sanguineo-notata, tubo turgido, limbo patenti-recurvo 5-lobo, staminibus 10, filamentis glabris, stigmate capitato vix exserto, ovario glanduloso-pubescente albido 10-loculari, capsula glaberrima lineari-cylindracea curva, valvis lignosis, seminibus atro-fuscis.

HAB. Sikkim-Himalaya; wooded valleys and on spurs of all the mountains, elev. 12-14,000 feet; abundant. *Fl.* June; *fr.* November.

A small shrubby *tree*, yielding to none in the beauty of its inflorescence amongst that yellow-flowered groupe of which it is the pride. The *trunks* are as thick as the thigh in the large specimens, and branch very much both upwards and outwards, forming a thickset shrub of ten feet high. *Ramuli* very thick and woody, the ultimate ones puberulous. *Petioles* half an inch long, stout, puberulous. *Leaf* six to eight (rarely ten) inches long, two and a half to three broad, very coriaceous, more plane than is usual in the genus, of a deep bright green above and but hardly glossy, beneath covered with a very closely appressed opaque tomentum of a more or less deep rufous colour, rarely pale and nearly white in the young foliage. *Capitula* much larger than those of *R. arboreum*, twelve- to twenty-flowered, but the flowers are not densely packed. *Bracteal scales* chestnut-brown, very coriaceous and viscid. *Pedicels* one inch to one and a half inch long, slender for the size of the flower. *Corolla* large and very beautiful, truly bell-shaped, being broad at the base and spherical, five-lobed at the insertion of the pedicel. *Capsules* nearly two inches long, ten-furrowed. Flowers have a faint honeyed smell; foliage inodorous.

This exceedingly handsome and abundant species replaces the *R. Hodgsoni* in ascending the mountains, and is the most prevalent species at 12 and 13,000 feet, conspicuous at all seasons for the large foliage, of a rusty cinnamon-colour underneath, and the viscid buds. It bears the name of a distinguished Indian botanist and personal friend, to whose zeal and liberality the botanists of India are no less publicly, than I am personally, indebted for encouragement and the most material aid in our common pursuits. The 'Icones Plantarum Indiæ Orientalis'—an excellent work in all respects, and indispensable to a knowledge of Indian plants—is a remarkable instance of the perfection to which botanical illustrations can be brought by indomitable perseverance under the most discouraging circumstances. The first plates of that work are equal to any produced at the era of their publication in India; the latter will compete with the best outline lithographs of Europe.

TAB. XXVII. *Rhododendron Wightii.* Fig. 1. Flower. 2. Stamen. 3. Peduncle, calyx, and pistil. 4. Transverse section of ovarium:—*magnified.* 5. Fruit:—*natural size.*

Tab. XXVIII

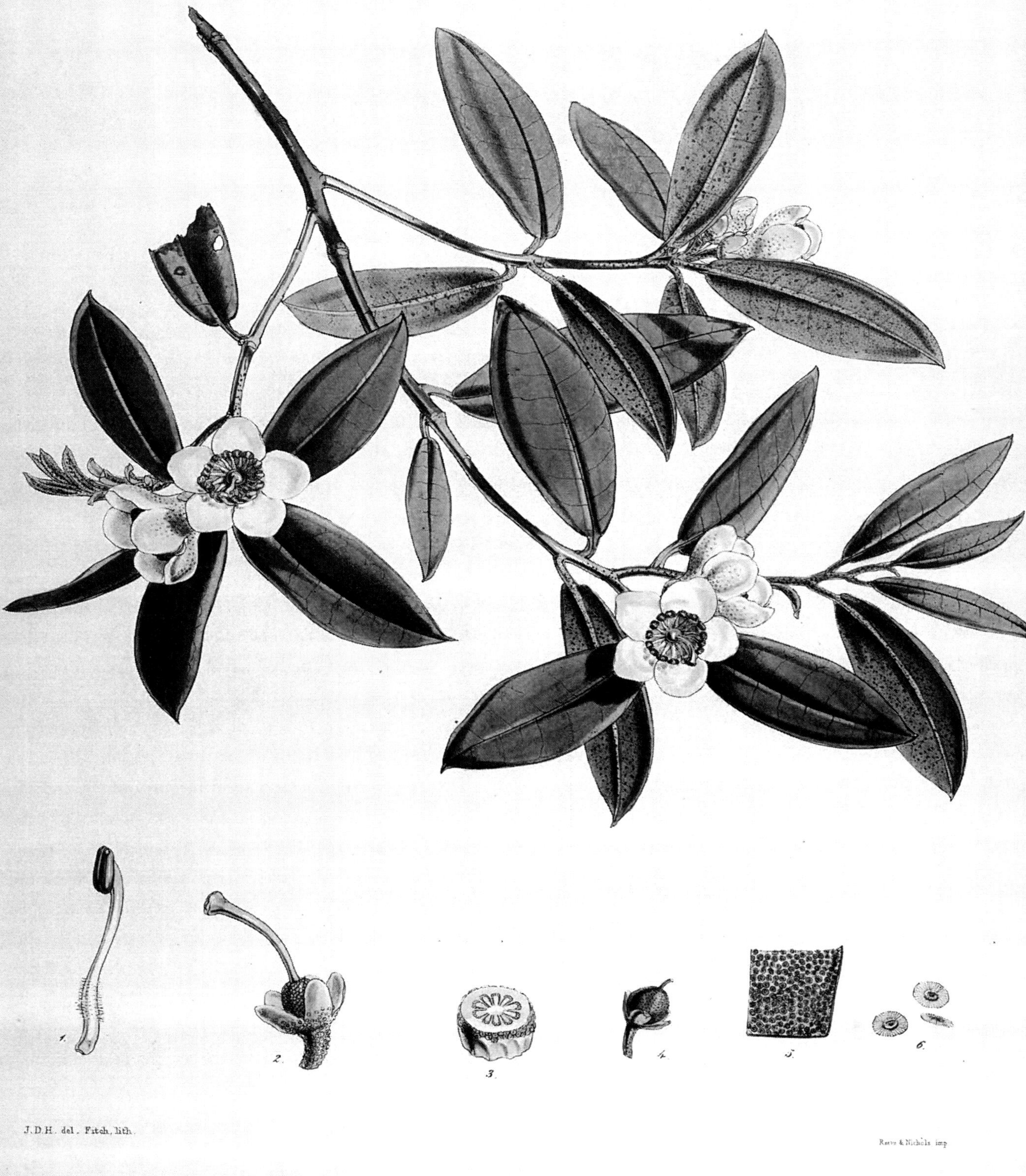

J.D.H. del. Fitch, lith.

Reeve & Nichols imp.

RHODODENDRON CAMELLIÆFLORUM, Hook. fil.

31.

RHODODENDRON CAMELLIÆFLORUM, *Hook. fil.*

Camellia-flowered Rhododendron.

TAB. XXVIII.

Frutex plerumque epiphytus, pendulus, laxus, parce ramosus, ramulis pedunculis petiolis foliisque subtus (junioribus utrinque) dense lepidoto-squamulosis ferrugineis, foliis petiolatis ellipticis utrinque acutis acuminatis muticisve, costa valida percursa, pedunculis brevissimis axillaribus solitariis, calycis lobis appressis rotundatis coriaceis, corolla carnosa, tubo brevi basi globoso, lobis patentibus orbicularibus, staminibus 16 radiatis, filamentis crassis, antheris majusculis, stylo crasso decurvo, ovario glabro 10-loculari, capsula brevi oblonga 10-loculari.

HAB. Sikkim-Himalaya; pendulous, generally from trunks of trees, often of Pines, sometimes from rocks, not unfrequent; elev. 9–11,000 feet. *Fl.* July; *fr.* December.

This very abnormal species is more allied, in some respects, to the section including *R. lepidotum,* than to any of the others: in foliage it resembles *R. Maddeni,* though so much smaller a plant, and also *R. cinnabarinum,* from which the dried flowerless specimens are not easily separable. The same very stout percurrent costa of the leaf is common to all these.

Stems two to six feet long, seldom thicker than a goose-quill, branches long, generally pendulous, though when growing on cliffs often obscurely so. *Leaves,* as usual in the genus, at the apices of the branches, differing in little but the size from those of *R. Maddeni,* two and a half to three inches long. *Peduncles* axillary or terminal, very short and stout. *Calyx* half the length of the tube of the corolla, very coriaceous, lepidote, one or more lobes at times lengthened and membranous. *Corolla* sparingly lepidote, an inch and a half across, of a very thick texture, pure white with a faint rosy tinge, all the segments obtuse and entire. *Stamens* very large for the size of the corolla: *filaments* incrassated and hairy at the base, also thickened below the *anther,* which is remarkably adnate and large, orange-red. *Ovarium* short, white with lepidote squamulæ. *Style* very stout, decurved, gradually enlarging to the abrupt disciform stigma. *Capsule* woody, broad, squamulose, obtuse at both ends, three inches and a quarter long; often diseased, and then spherical (fig. 4). The similarity between the flower and that of a single (wild) *Camellia* has suggested the trivial name. Odour, as in all the lepidote species, more or less strongly resinous according to the heat of the day.

TAB. XXVIII. *Rhododendron camelliæflorum.* Fig. 1. Stamen. 2. Peduncle, calyx, and pistil. 3. Transverse section of ovarium. 4. Fruit, diseased. 5. Portion of under side of leaf. 6. Squamulæ from the same:—*all except figure 4 magnified.*

Tab. XXIX.

J.D.H. del. Fitch, lith.

Reeve & Nichols, imp.

RHODODENDRON CANDELABRUM, Hook. fil.

32.

RHODODENDRON CANDELABRUM, *Hook. fil.*

Candelabra Rhododendron.

Tab. XXIX.

Frutex ramosissimus, foliis terminalibus subcoriaceis glaberrimis oblongo-ovatis obtusissimis apiculatis basi cordatis subtus glaucescentibus margine subrecurvo, corymbis plurifloris, pedunculis petiolo æquantibus, floribus radiatim patentibus cernuisve, calyce brevi disciformi obscure inæqualiter lobato ciliato, corolla pallide rosea, tubo elongato campanulato, limbo 5-lobo, staminibus 10, ovario conico-cylindraceo glanduloso-ciliato.

Hab. Sikkim-Himalaya; elev. 10–11,000 feet. *Fl.* June.

The plant from which the accompanying plate and description are taken, was found in thick Pine-woods near Lachen village, before I was well acquainted with the *R. Thomsoni* (Tab. XII.), of which I fear it is only a pale-flowered variety, found growing at a lower elevation than that species usually inhabits, flowering earlier and in a shady protected situation. The much shorter calyx (of the same peculiar character, however), its glandular margin and ovarium, are the only further distinctions I have been able to detect between them, and they are quite unimportant.

Tab. XXIX. *Rhododendron candelabrum.* Fig. 1. Stamen. 2. Peduncle, calyx, and pistil. 3. Transverse section of ovary:—*all magnified.*

Tab. XXX

J.D.H. del. Fitch, lith.

Reeve & Nichols imp.

RHODODENDRON CAMPYLOCARPUM. Hook. fil.

33.

RHODODENDRON CAMPYLOCARPUM, *Hook. fil.*

Curve-fruited Rhododendron.

TAB. XXX.

Frutex gracilis, virgatus, ramosus, cortice papyraceo, ramulis ultimis pedunculis pedicellisque glanduloso-pilosis, foliis petiolatis ovato- vel oblongo-cordatis apice rotundatis utrinque glaberrimis superne nitidis subter pallidioribus interdum glaucescentibus, capitulis terminalibus laxis 6–8-floris, pedicellis gracilibus, calyce 5-lobo glanduloso, corolla (elegantissima) campanulata alba v. saturate straminea immaculata, lobis 5 patentibus, staminibus 10, antheris rubris, filamentis glabris, ovario glanduloso, capsulis patentibus valde arcuatis cylindraceis angustis pilis rigidis glanduloso-capitatis aspersis plerisque 6-valvis, seminibus pallidis.

HAB. Sikkim-Himalaya; rocky valleys and open spurs, elev. 11–14,000 feet; abundant. *Fl.* June; *fr.* November.

A small *bush*, averaging six feet in height, rounded in form, of a bright cheerful green hue, and which, when loaded with its inflorescence of surpassing delicacy and grace, claims precedence over its more gaudy congeners, and has always been regarded by me as the most charming of the Sikkim Rhododendrons. The plant exhales a grateful honeyed flavour from its lovely bells and a resinous sweet odour from the stipitate glands of the petioles, pedicels, calyx, and capsules. *Leaves* on slender petioles, three-quarters of an inch long, coriaceous but not thick in texture, two to three and a half inches long, one and three-quarters to two inches broad, cordate at the base, rounded and mucronate at the apex, in all characters, except the evanescent glandular pubescence and spherical buds, undistinguishable from *Rhododendron Thomsoni*. *Flowers* horizontal and nodding. *Corolla* truly campanulate, delicate in texture, tinged of a sulphur hue and always spotless, nearly two inches long, broader across the lobes, which are finely veined. The pedicels of the capsules radiate horizontally from the apices of the ramuli, and the capsules themselves curve upwards with a semicircular arc; they are about an inch long, always loosely covered with stipitate glands.

TAB. XXX. *Rhododendron campylocarpum.* Fig. 1. Stamen. 2. Peduncle, calyx, and pistil. 3. Transverse section of ovarium :—*magnified.* 4. Fruit :—*natural size.*